Burford Ontario and Area in Photos, Saving Our History One Photo at a Time

Photography
by Barbara Raué
2012

Series Name:
Cruising Ontario

Book 11: Burford and Area

Cover photo: Burford Post Office A.D. 1914

Series Name: Cruising Ontario

Other Books by Barbara Raue

Coins and Gems

Arrows, Indians and Love

The Life and Times of Barbara
Volume 1: Inventions That Have Enhanced My Life
Volume 2: Entertainment That I Have Enjoyed
Volume 3: East Coast Trip 2009
Volume 4: Olympics
Volume 5: Wonders of the World

Burford and Area

Burford, a rural community in the County of Brant, is located eight kilometres west of Brantford along Highway 53. In 1793, Lieutenant Governor Simcoe granted to Abraham Dayton the township of Burford. Dayton came with several other families from New Milford, Connecticut, USA and he settled west of the present village. When there was a high demand for tobacco, the farms and families surrounding Burford were prosperous, but when smoking habits were changing in the 1980s, the economy began to decline. Many farmers now grow ginseng for oriental markets. Dairy, poultry and pig farming continues with large scale commercial operations as well as family farms.

Mount Vernon is now a community of large modern homes.

Bishopsgate is another small community nearby. We found a few old buildings still in existence.

Burford Homes and Buildings

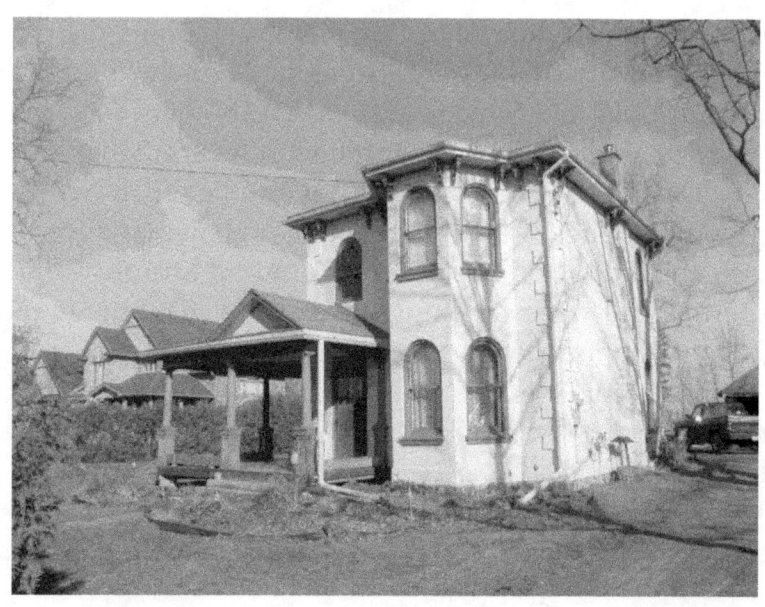

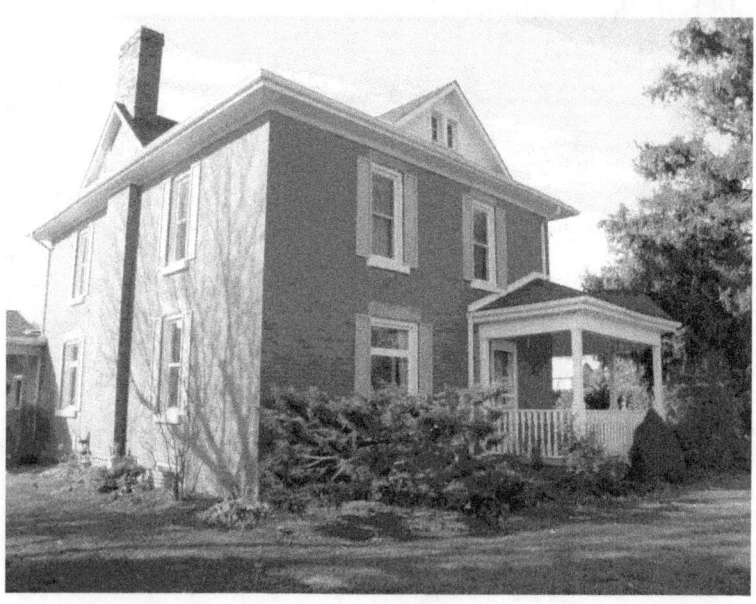

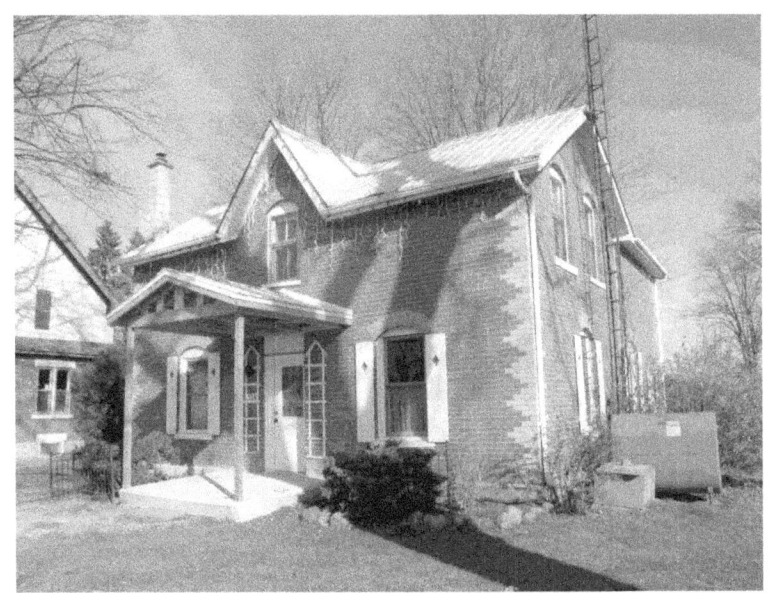

354 Maple Avenue

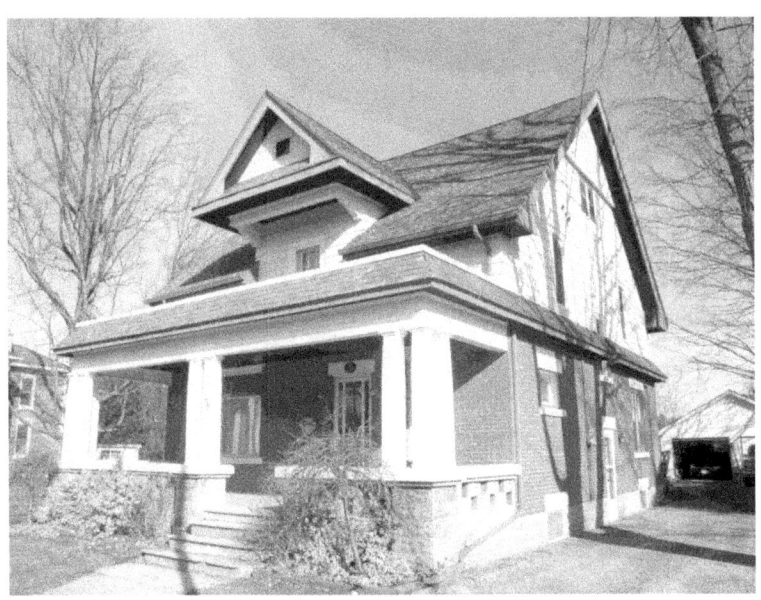

356 Maple Avenue

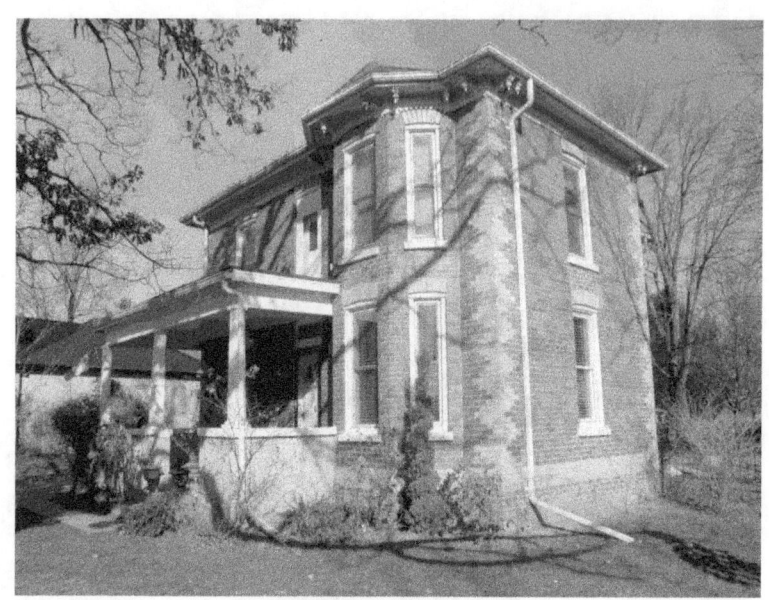

358 Maple Avenue

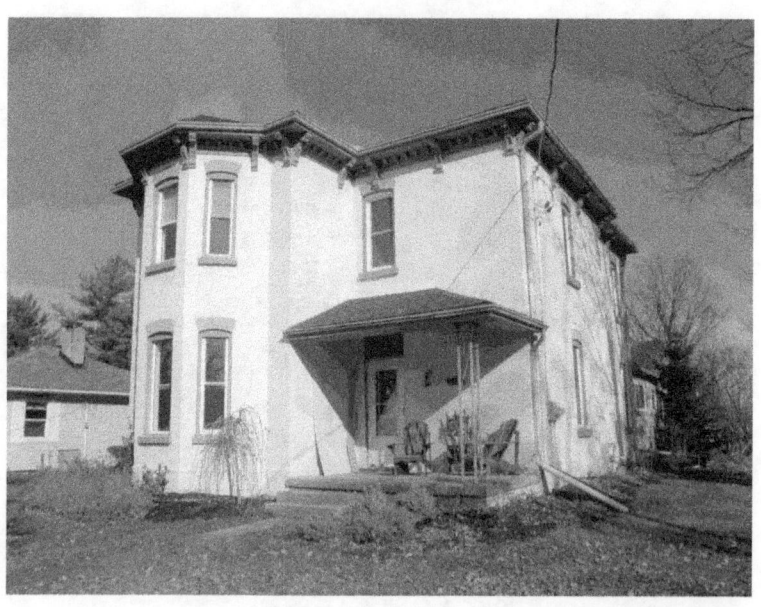

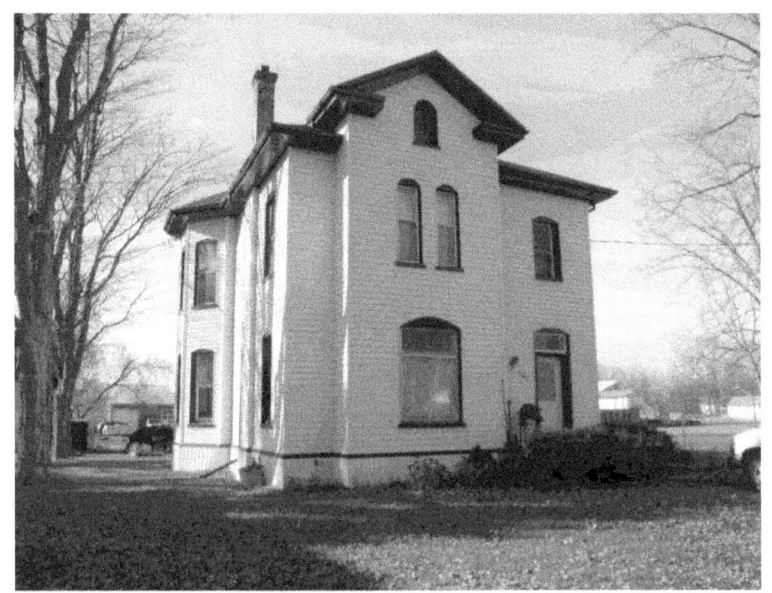

365 Maple Avenue

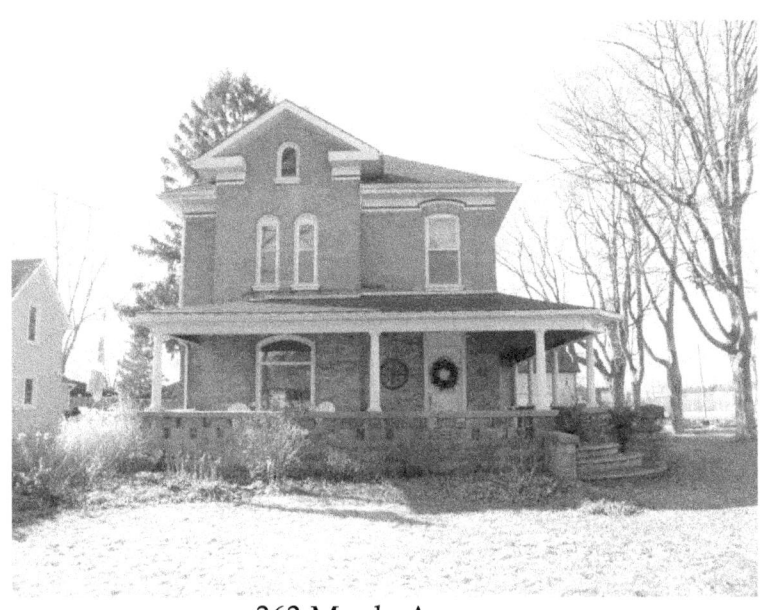

363 Maple Avenue

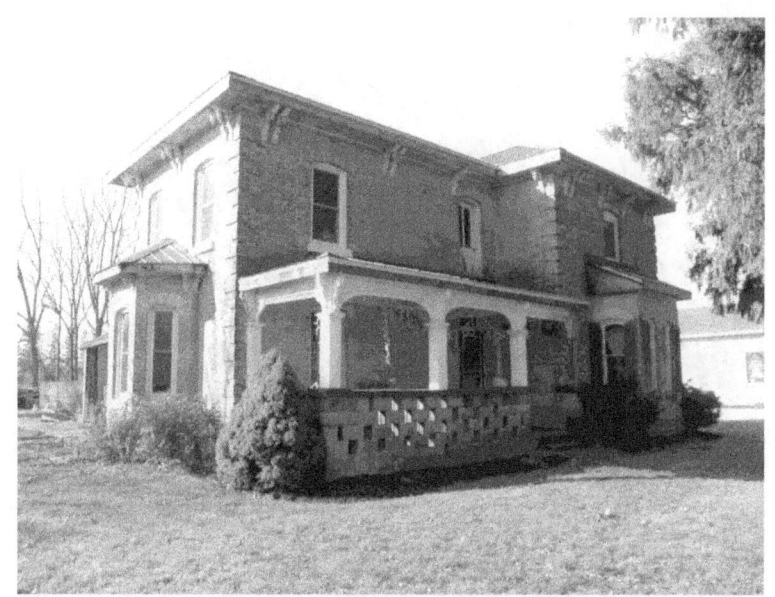

371 Maple Avenue

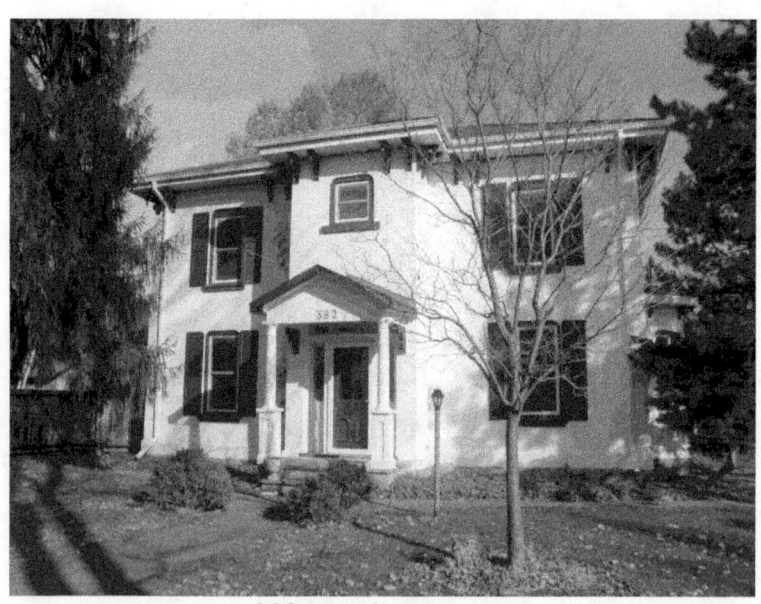

382 Maple Avenue

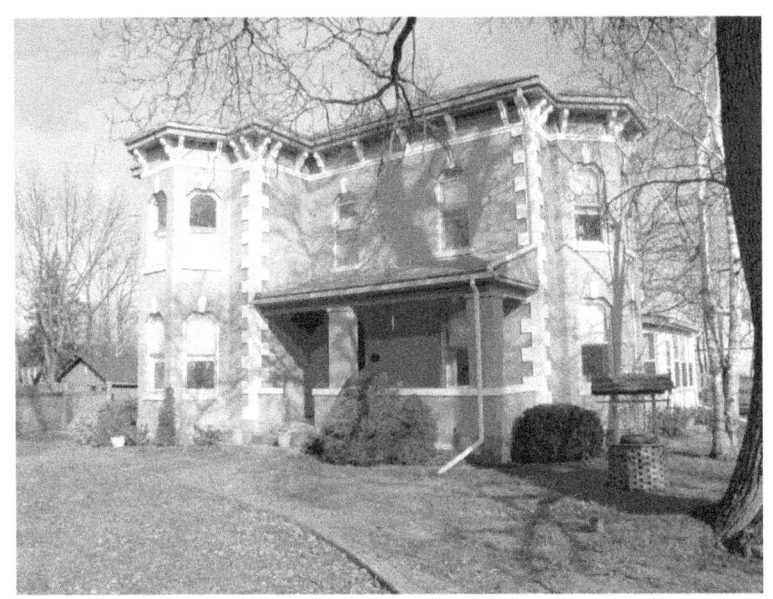

374 Maple Avenue
Heritage Property – c. 1875

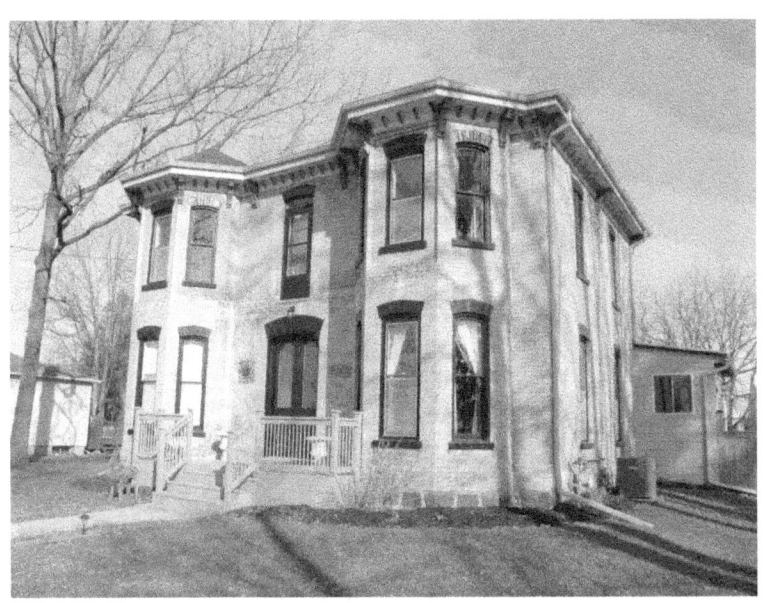

376 Maple Avenue
Yellow brick

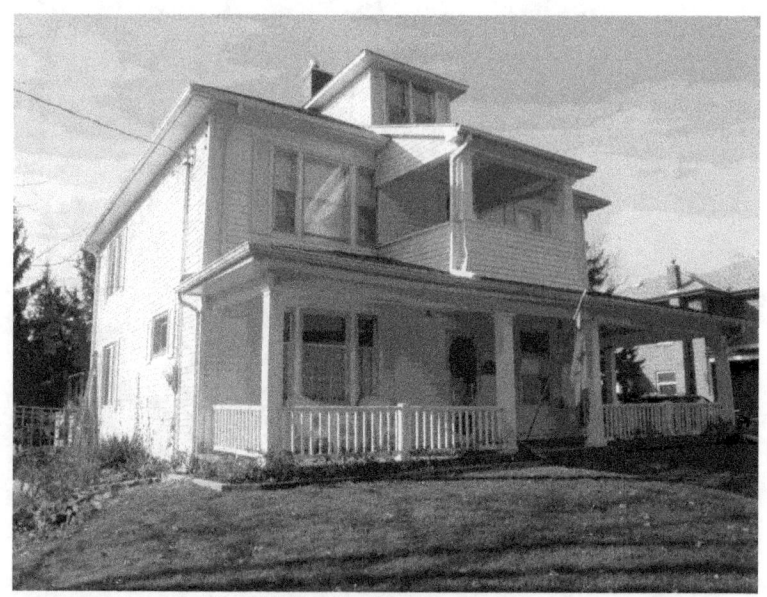

381 Maple Avenue

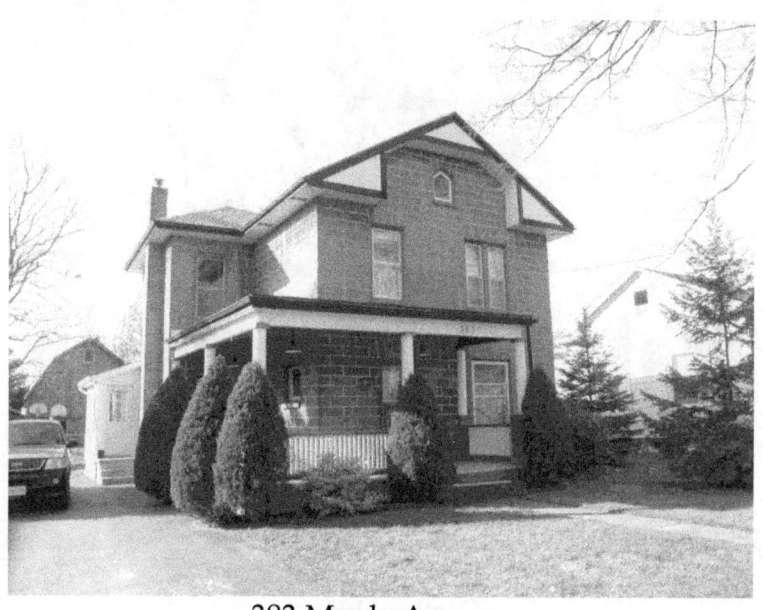

383 Maple Avenue

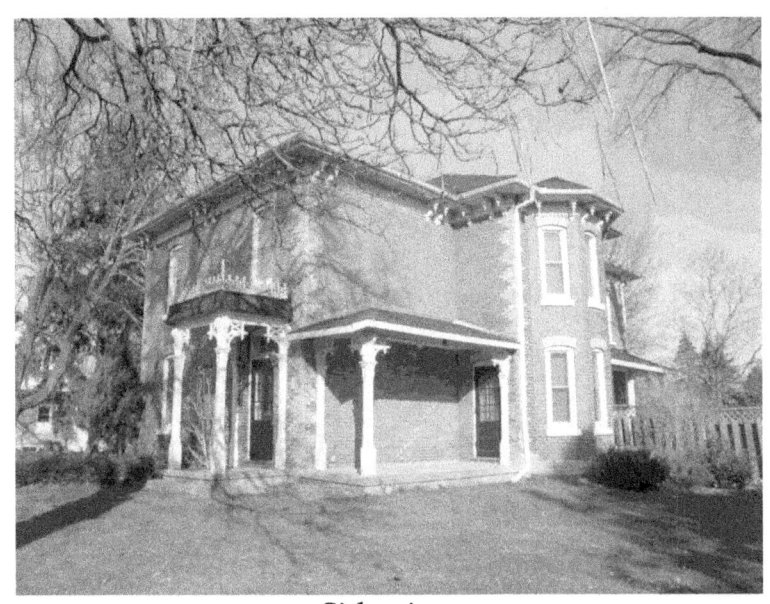

Side view
386 Maple Avenue
Two-tone brick accents, intricate ironwork around balcony
above front dooor

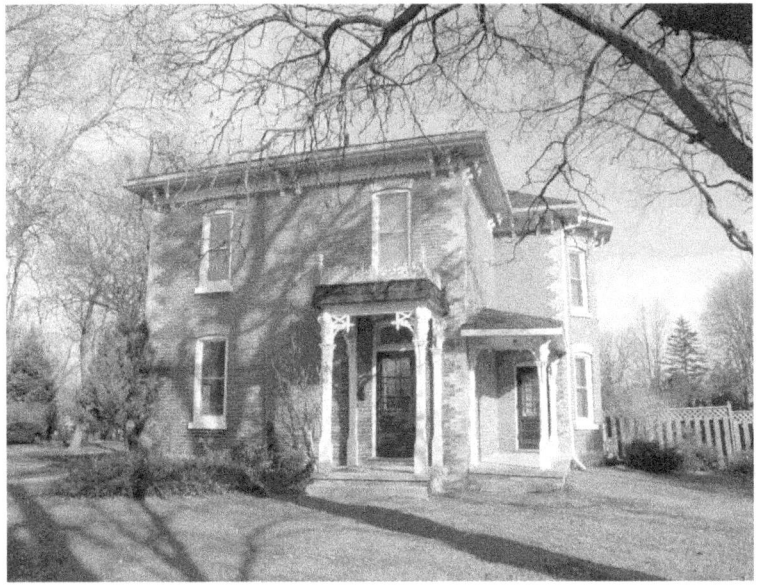

Front view

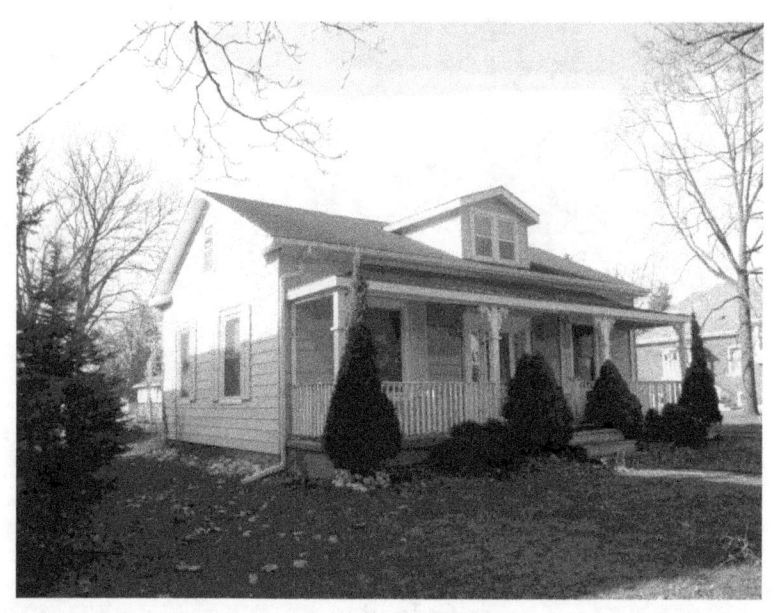

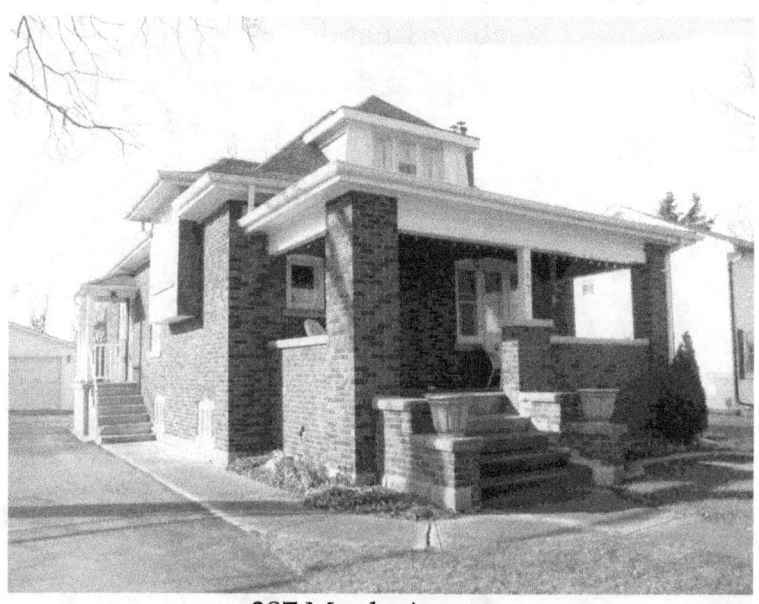

387 Maple Avenue

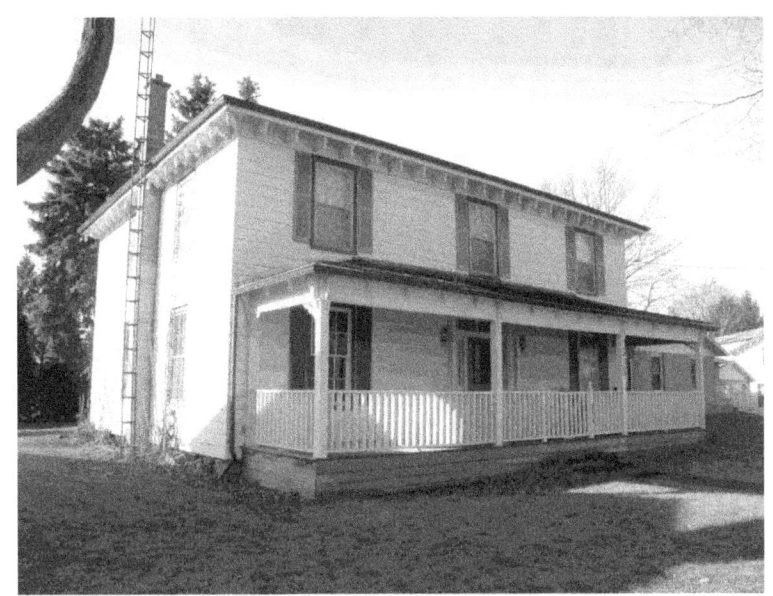

393 Maple Avenue

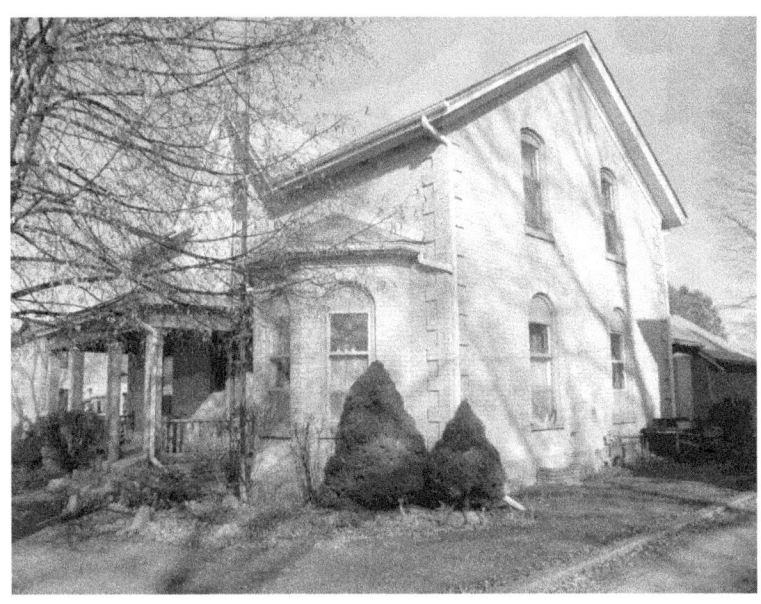

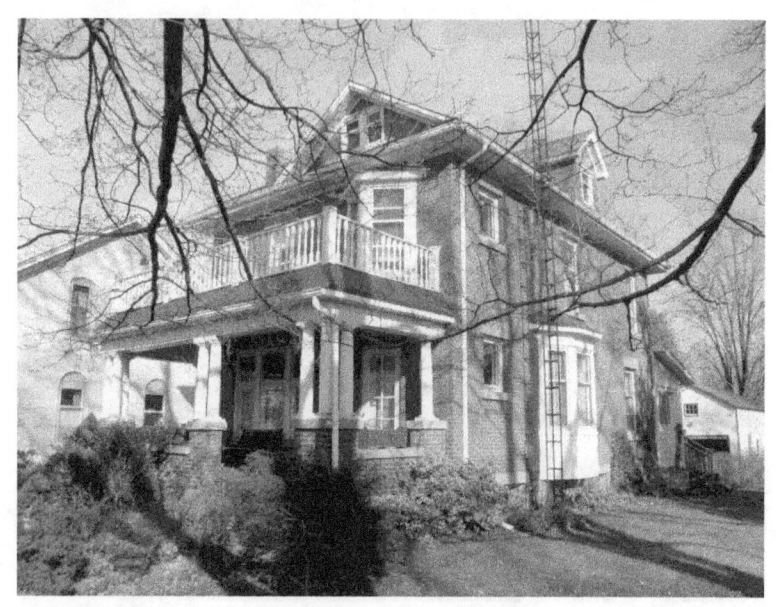

394 Maple Avenue

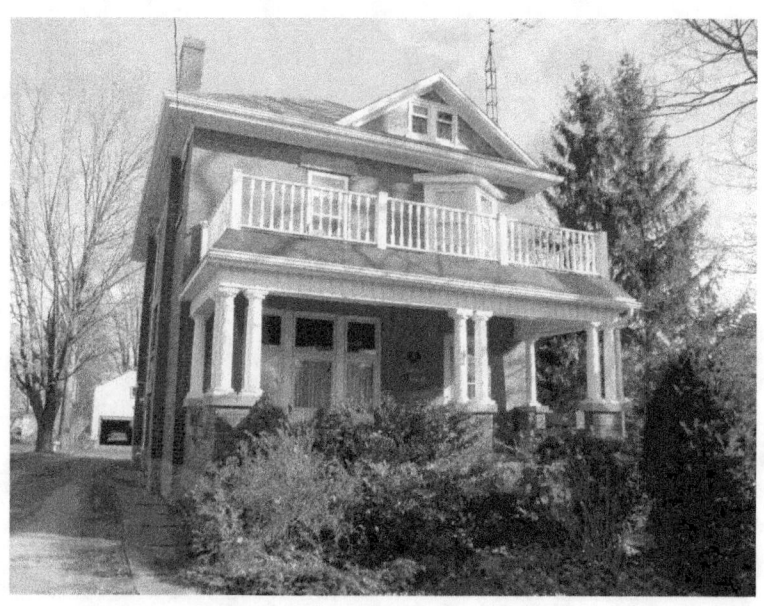

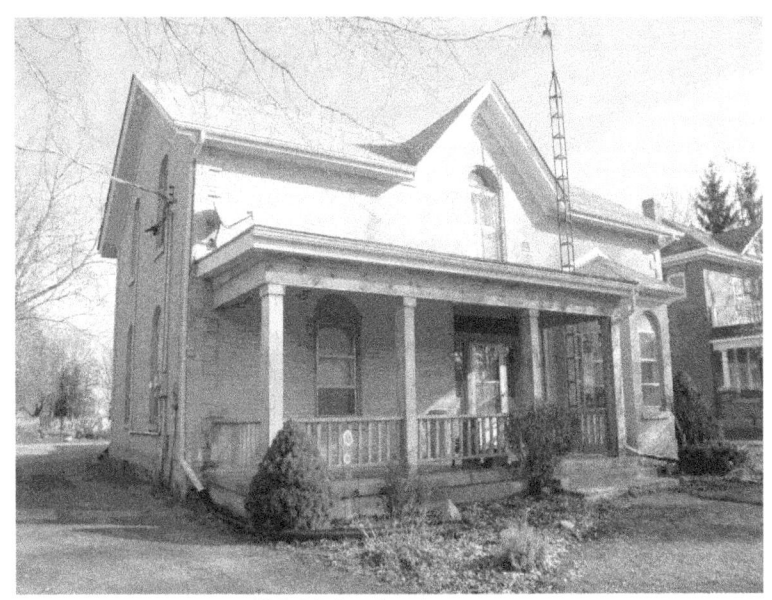

396 Maple Avenue

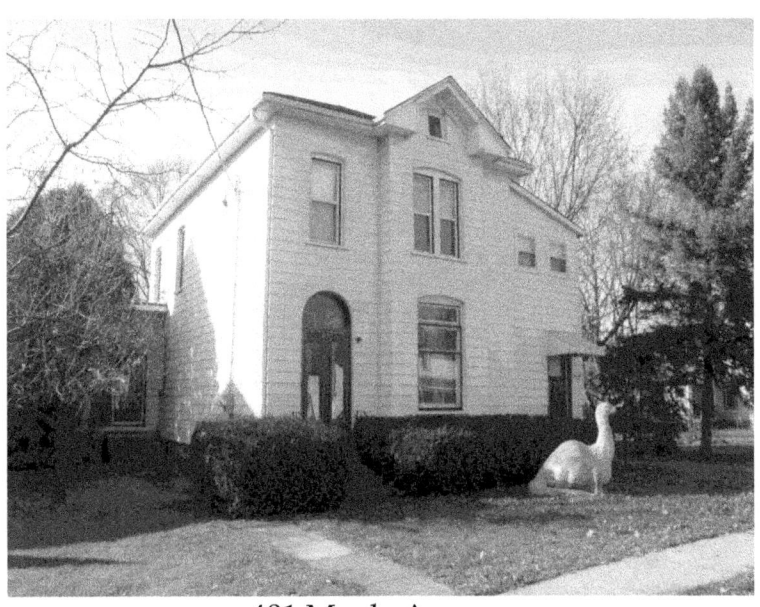

401 Maple Avenue

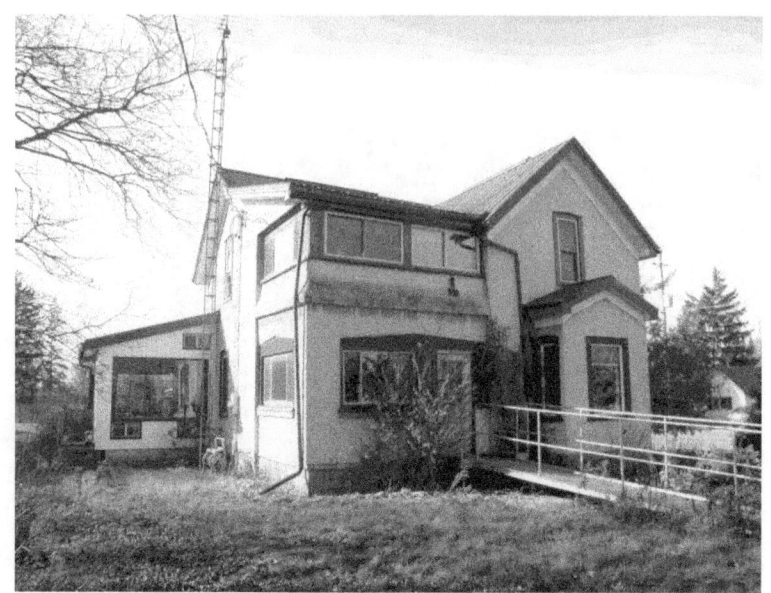

405 Maple Avenue

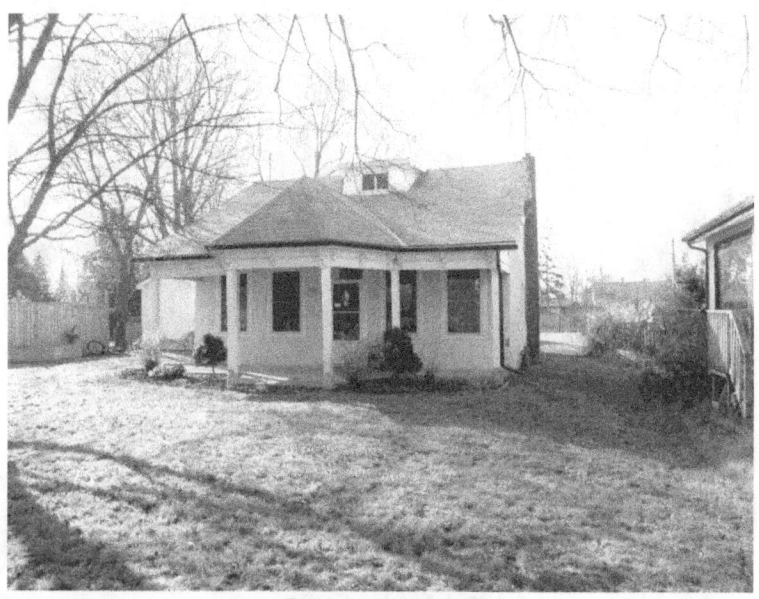

Stucco cottage

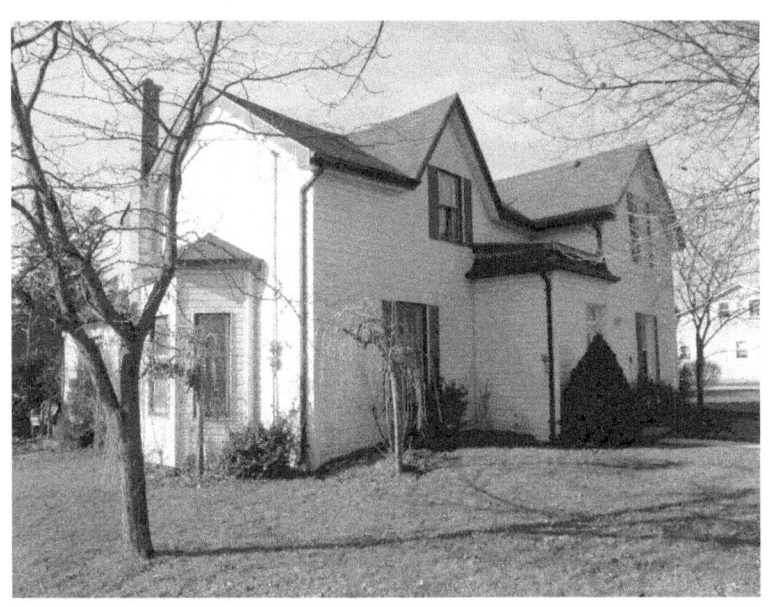

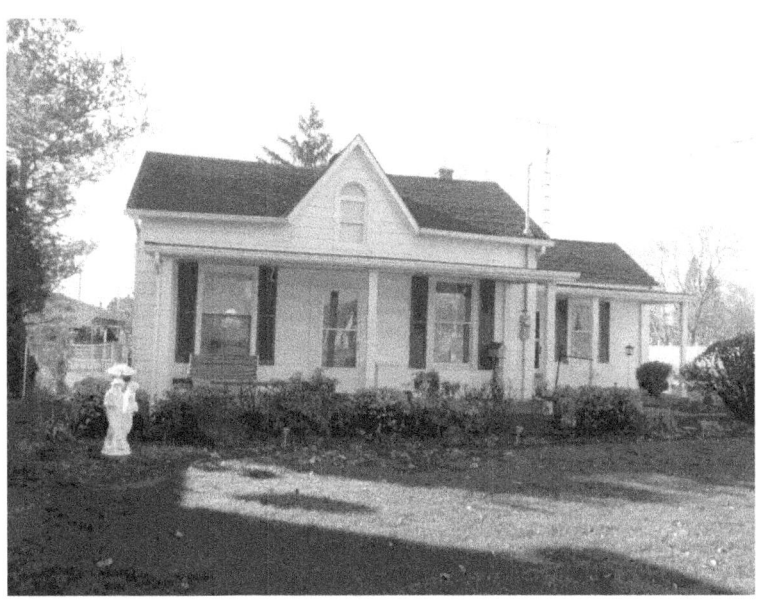

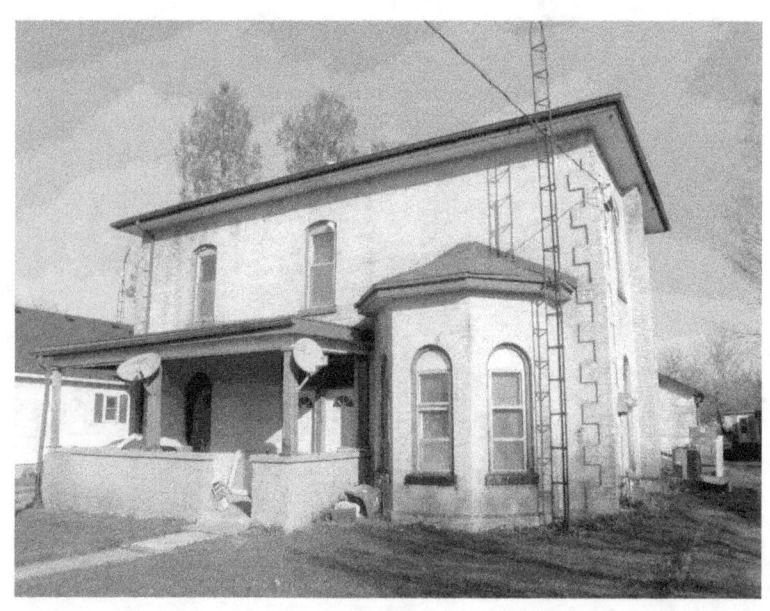

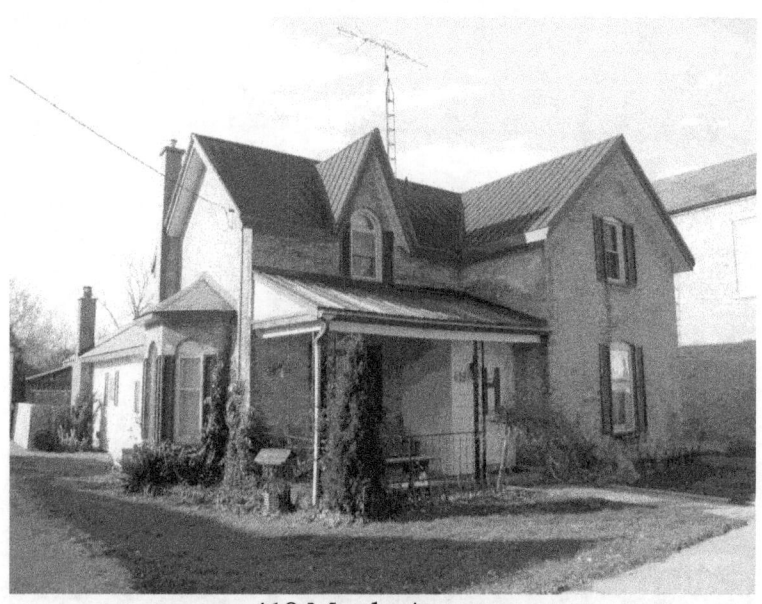

419 Maple Avenue

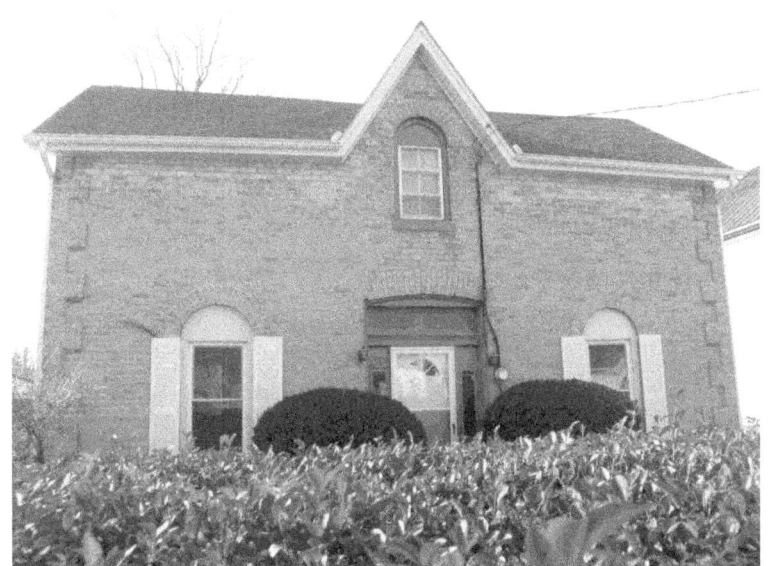

Gothic style arch

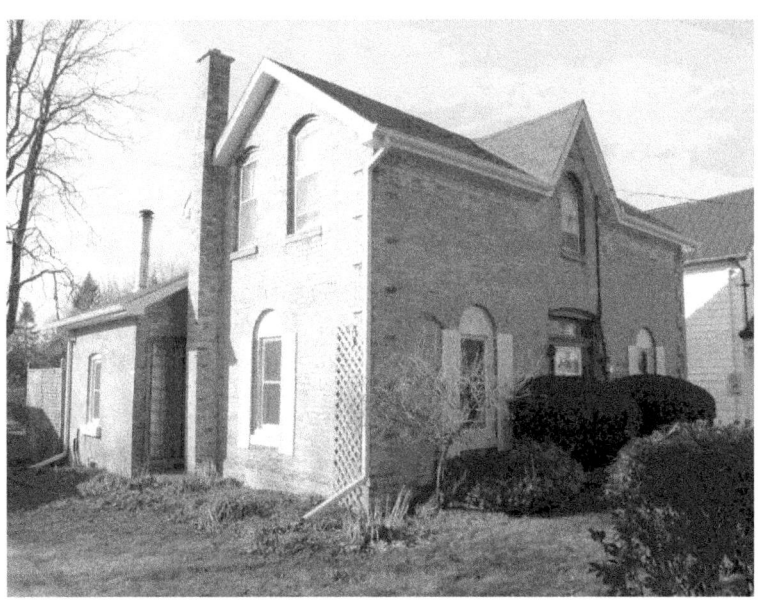

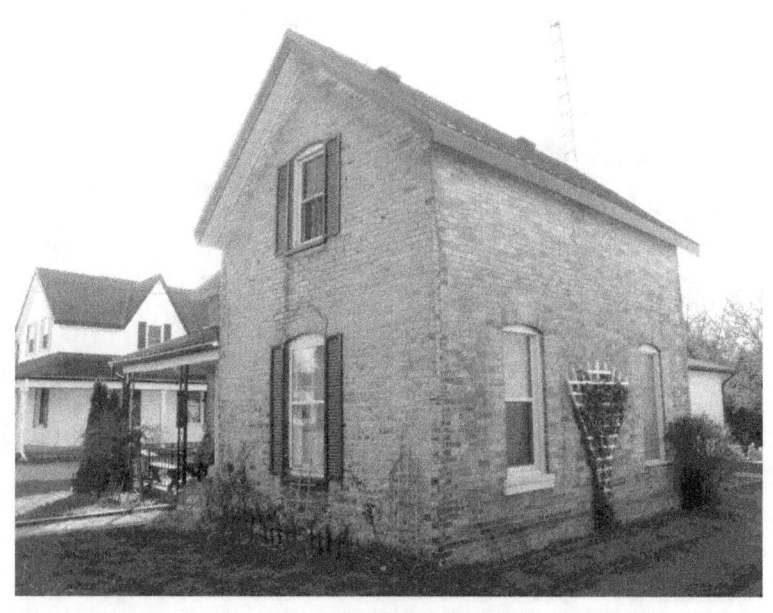

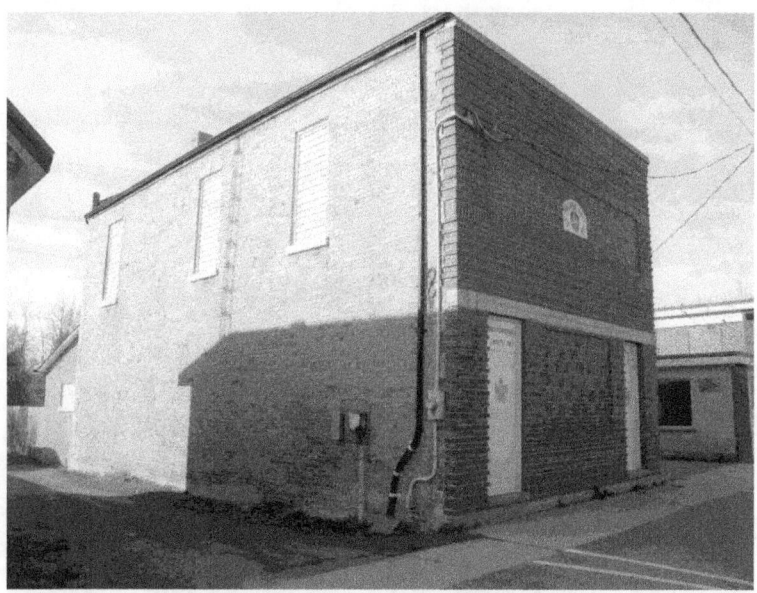

Masonic Hall 1883

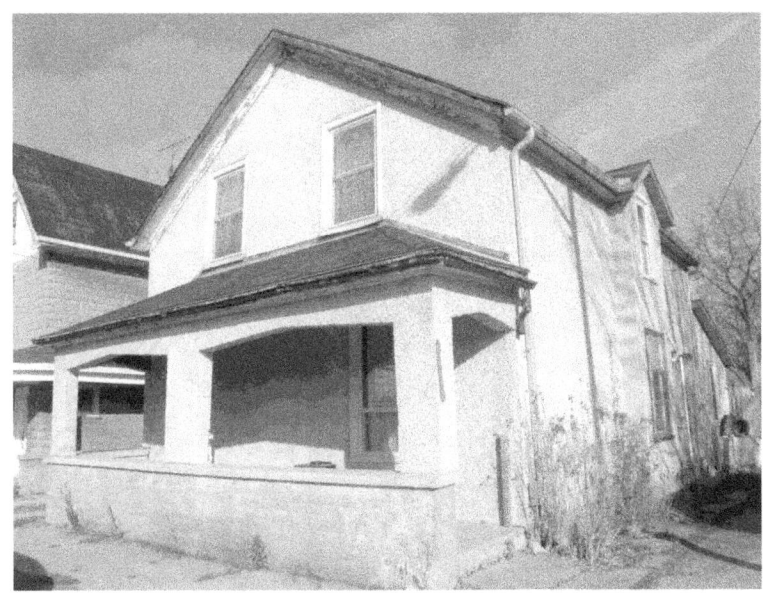

Stucco building

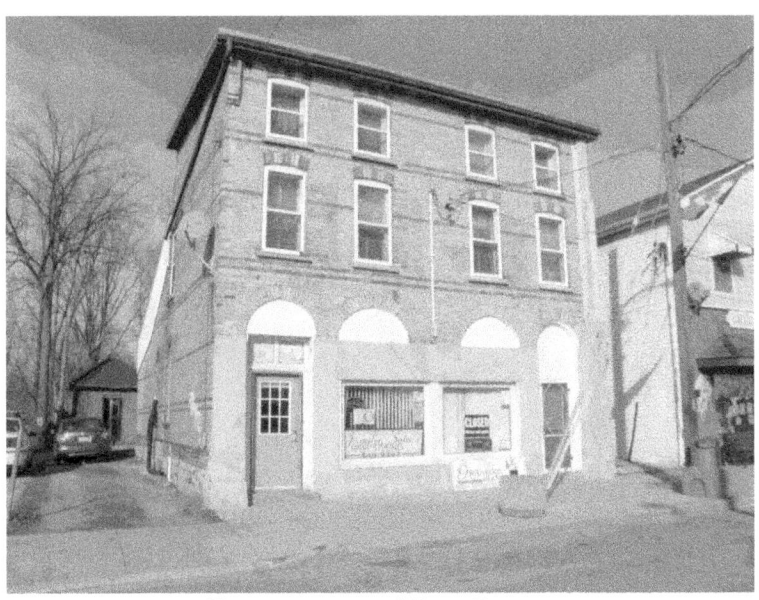

Downtown – King Street
Two-tone brickwork above the upper windows

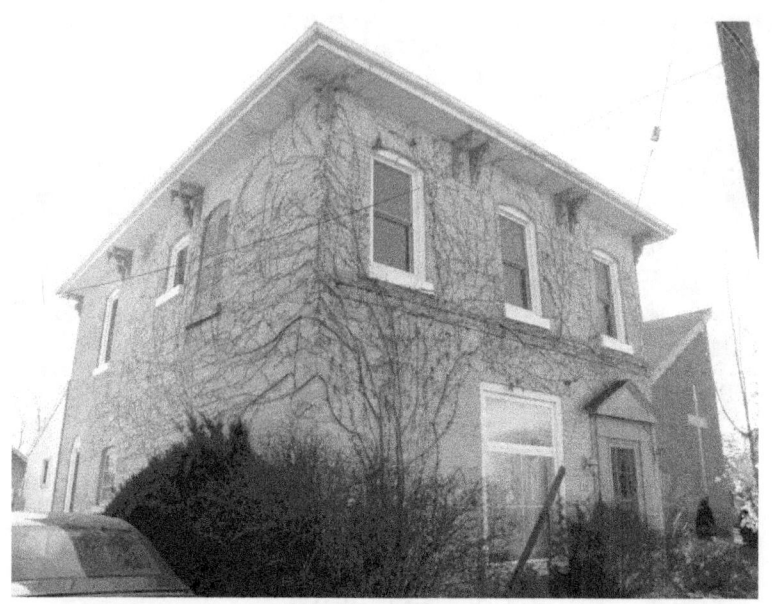

135 King Street

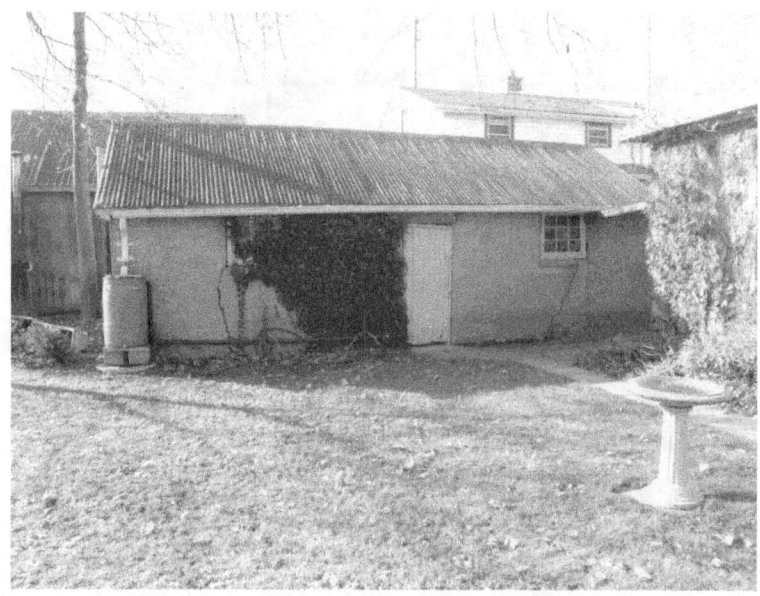

Old stone building on Alexander Street behind 139 King Street

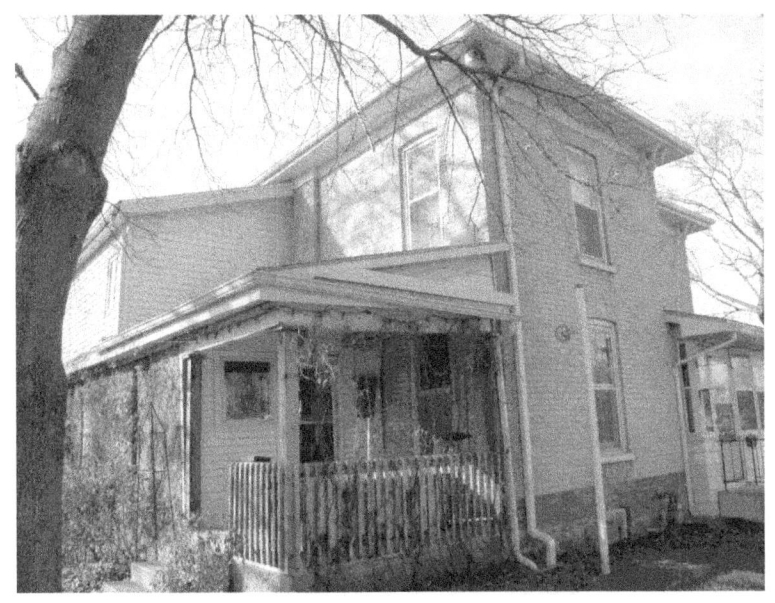

139 King Street on the corner of Alexander Street

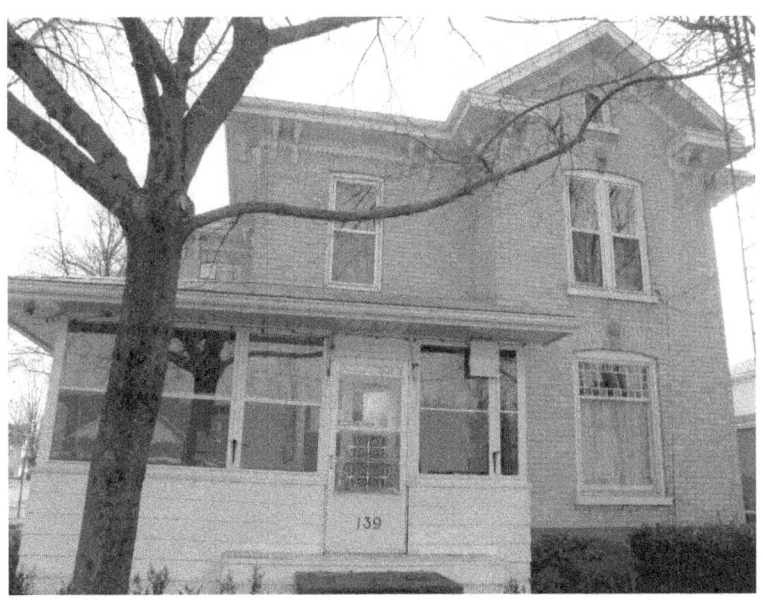

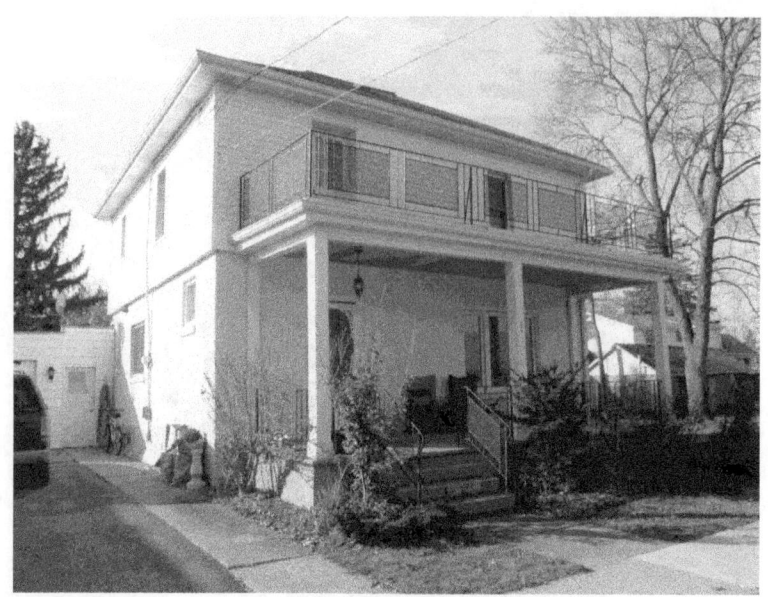

1 Alexander Street

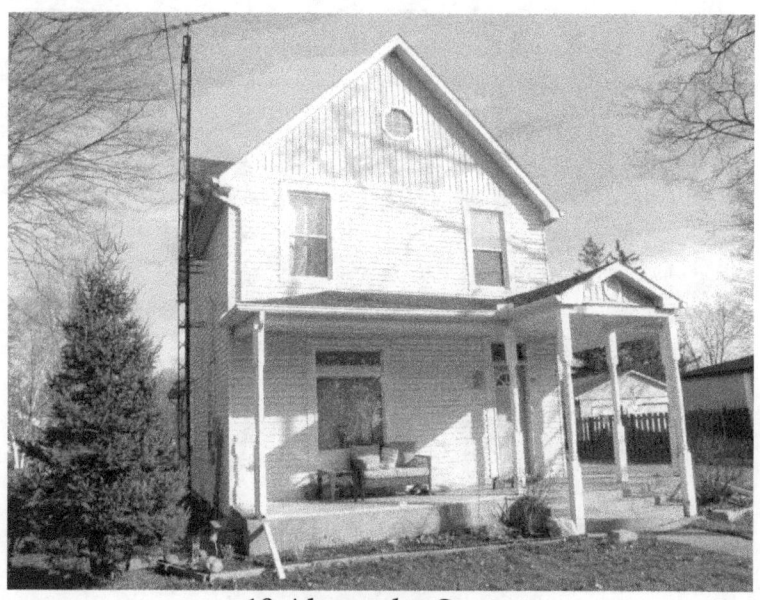

10 Alexander Street

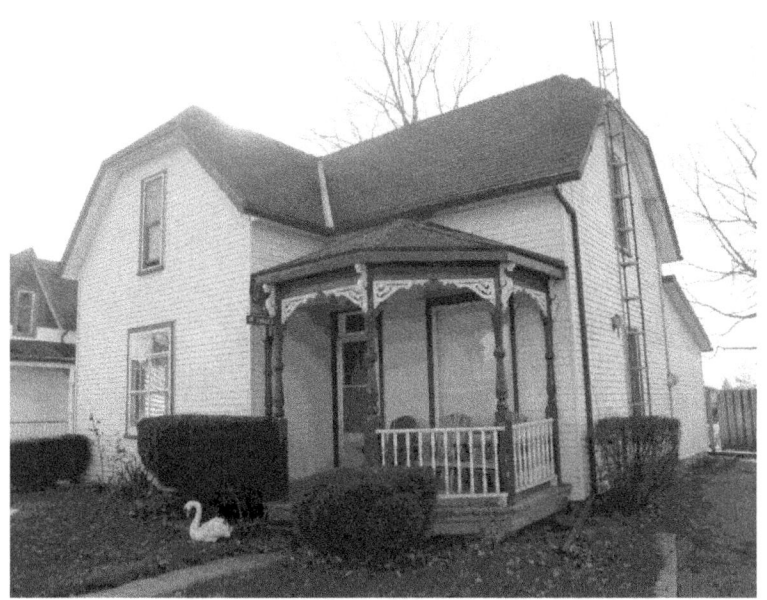

13 Alexander Street

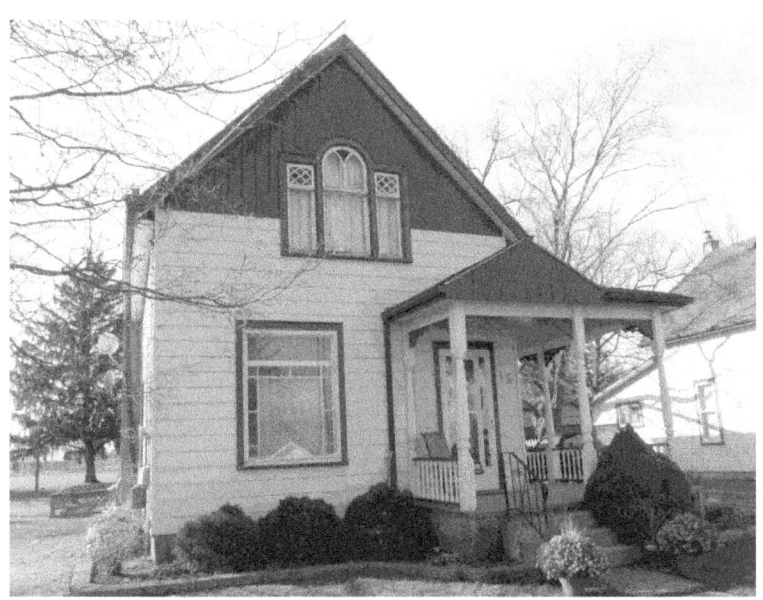

15 Alexander Street

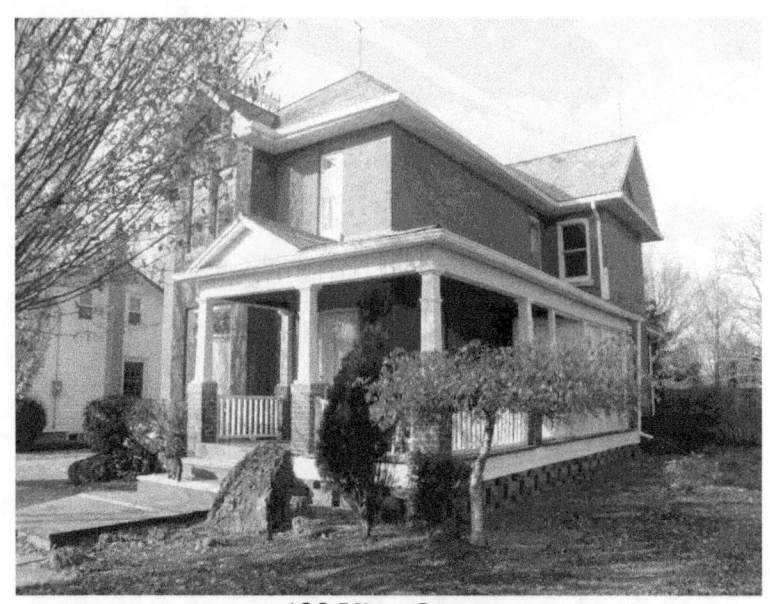

138 King Street
Heritage Property c. 1912

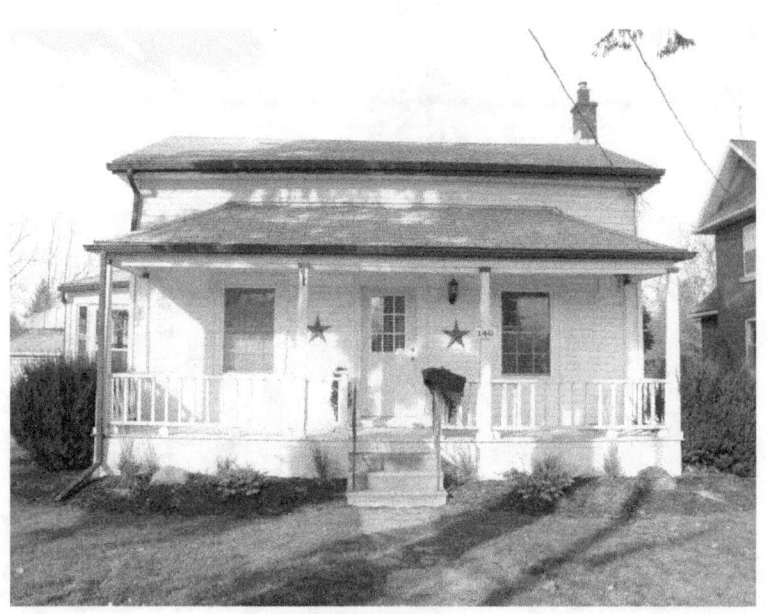

140 King Street

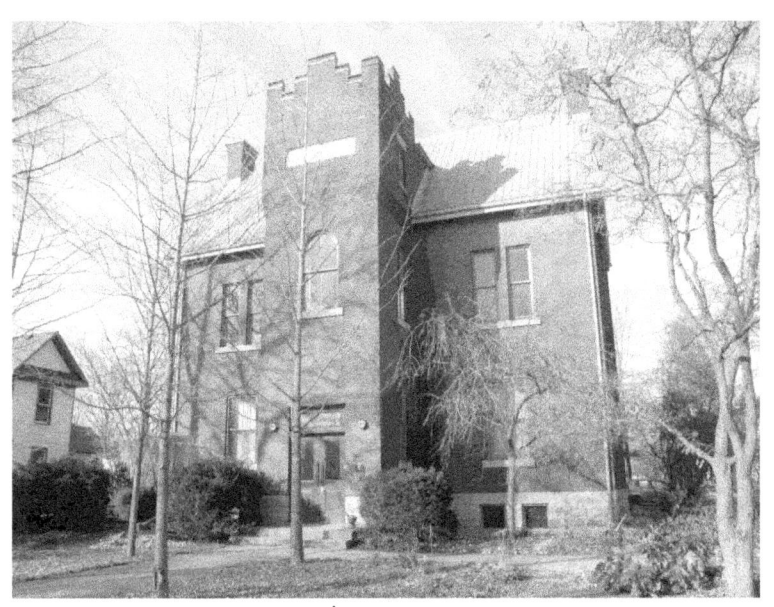

Armoury
Heritage Property built 1906
150 King Street

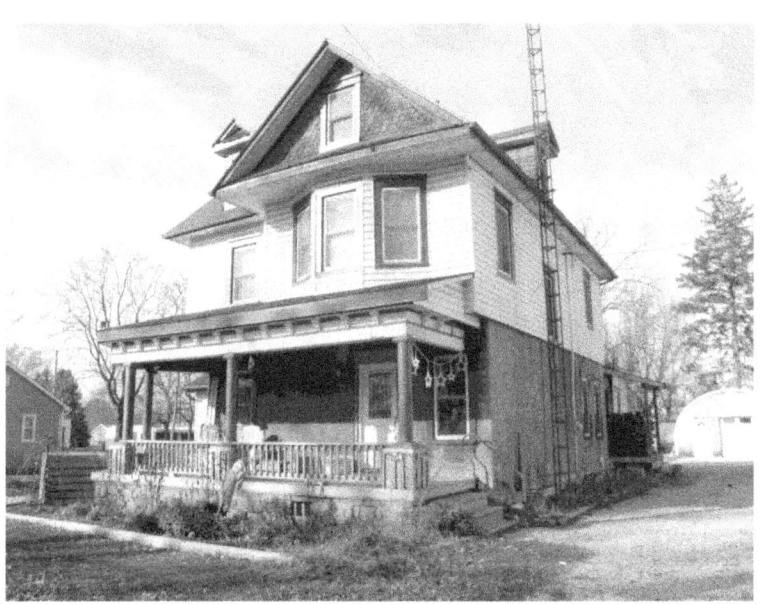

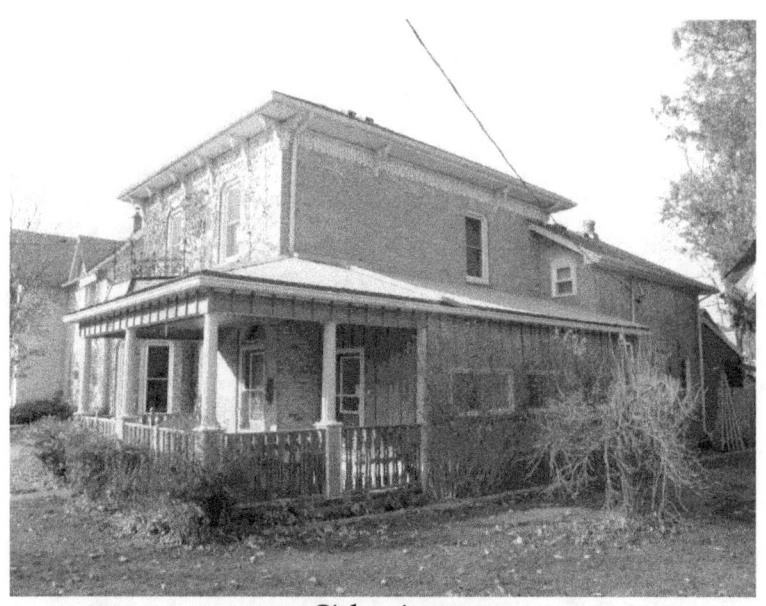

Side view
Fancy brackets under the eaves
146 King Street

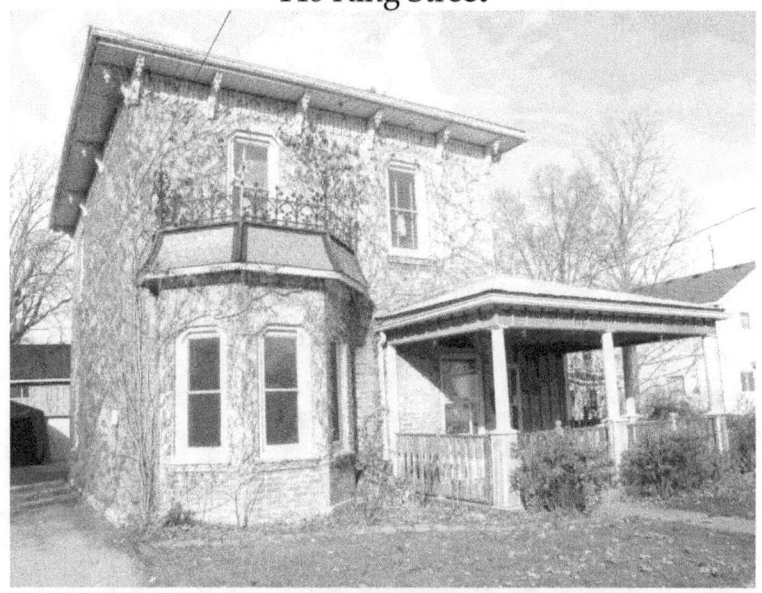

Front view
Intricate ironwork above the bay window

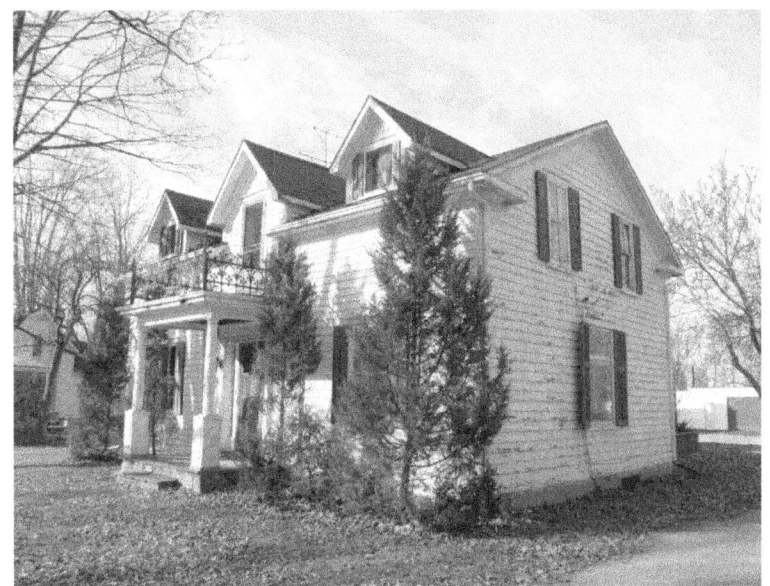

158 King Street

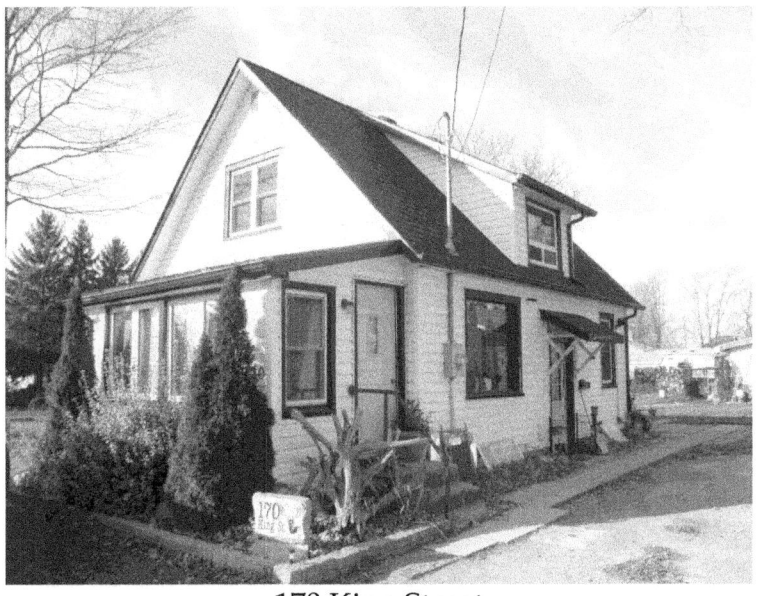

170 King Street

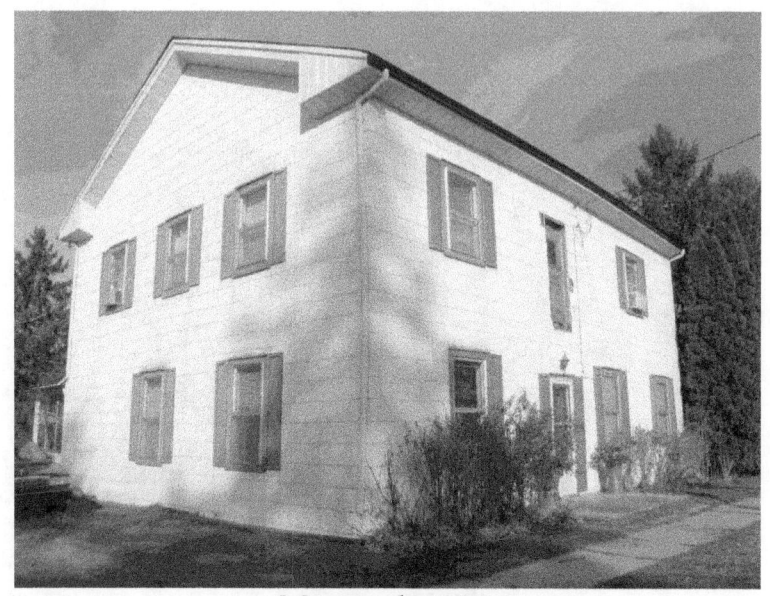

Mauve shutters

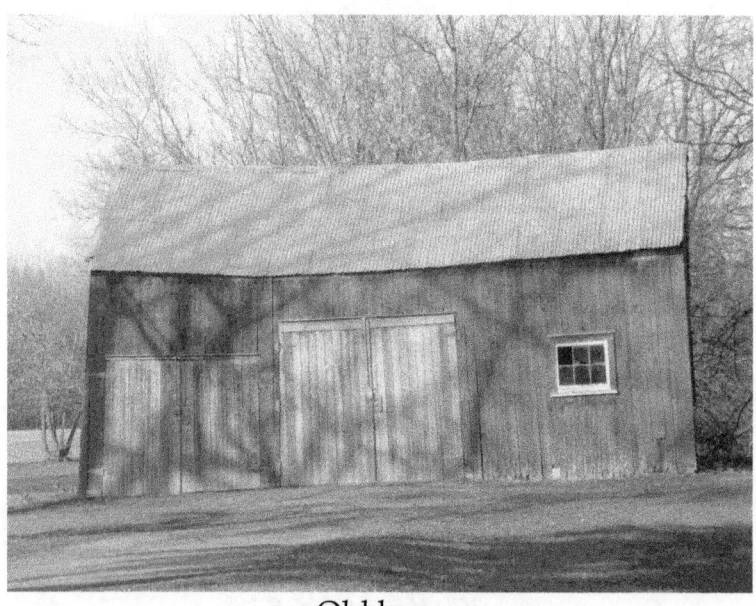

Old barn

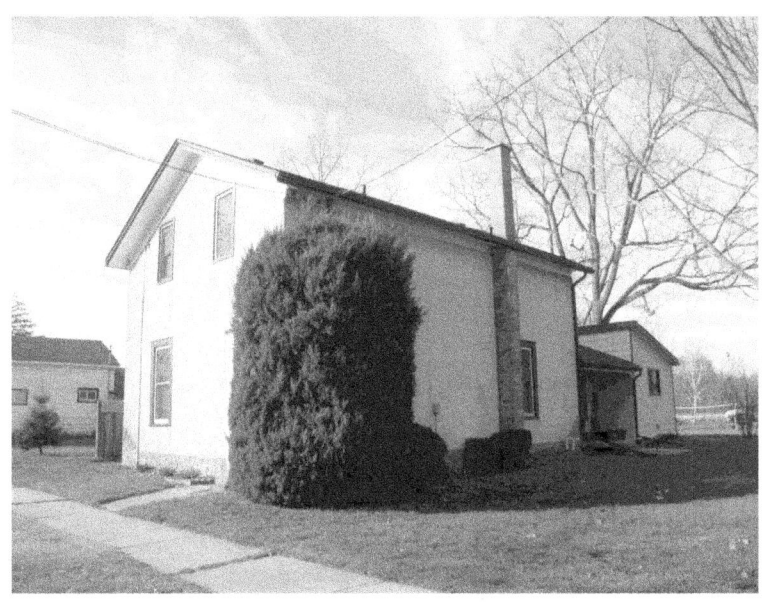

Stucco homes

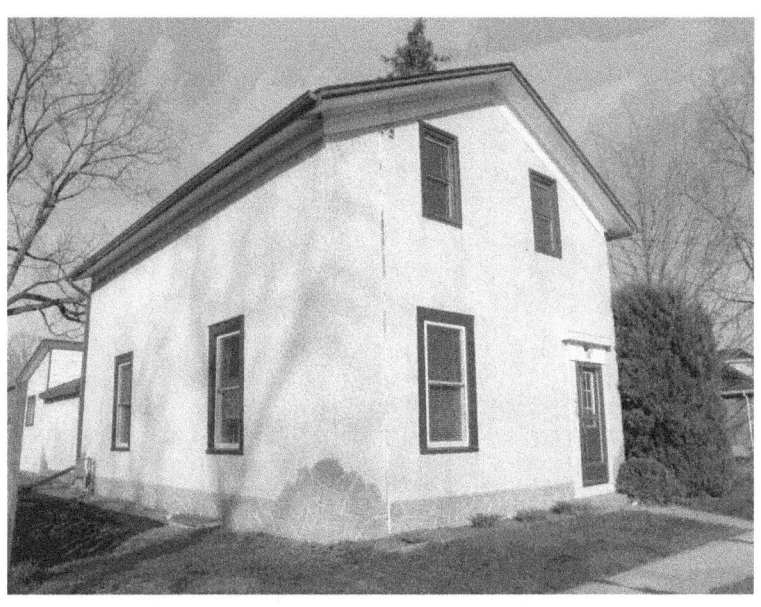

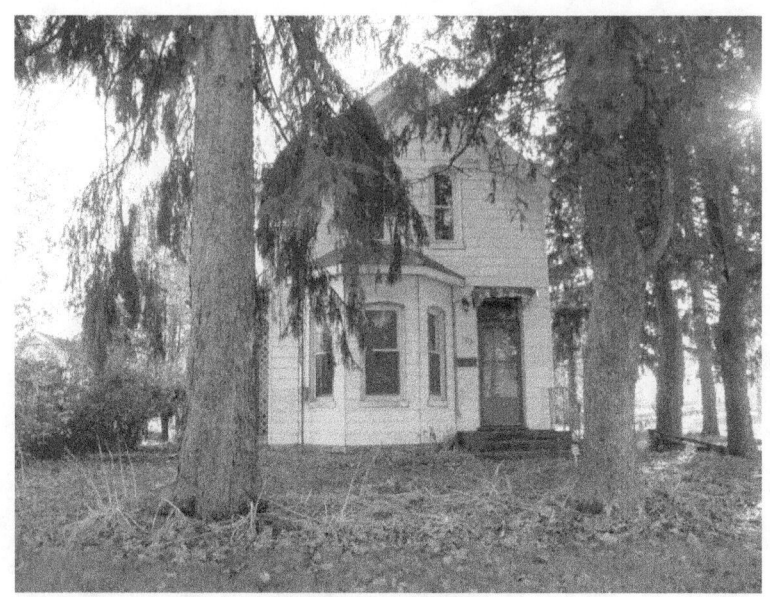

179 King Street
Partially hidden among the pines

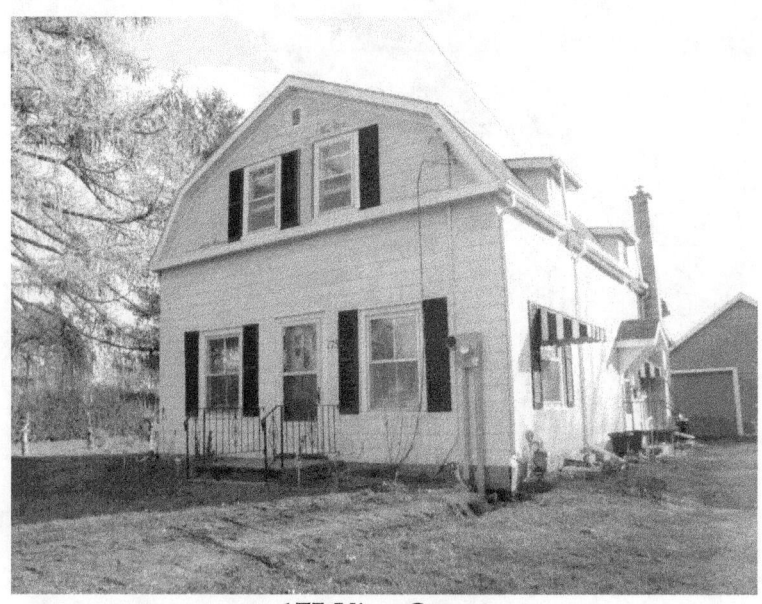

175 King Street

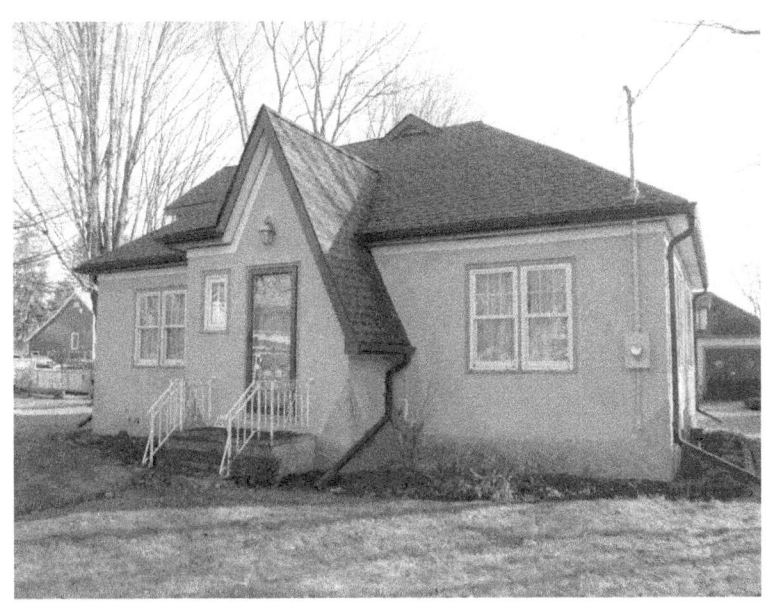

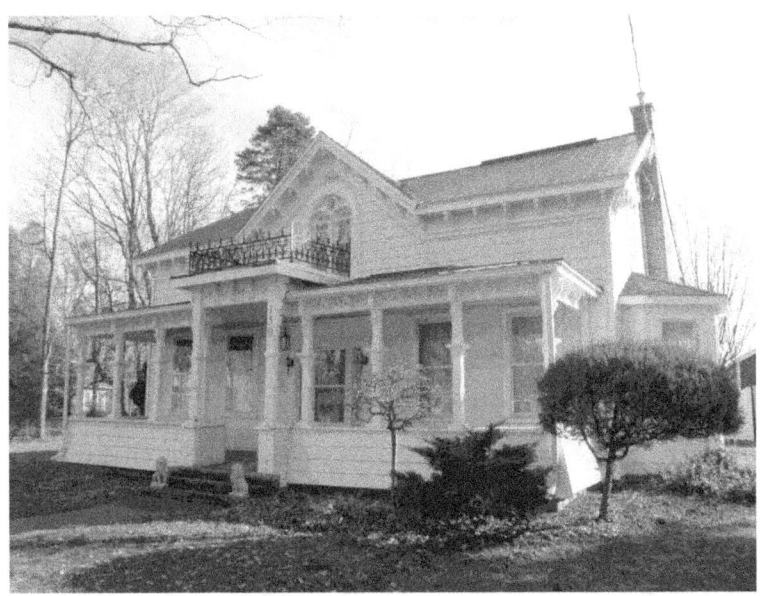

159 King Street c. 1888

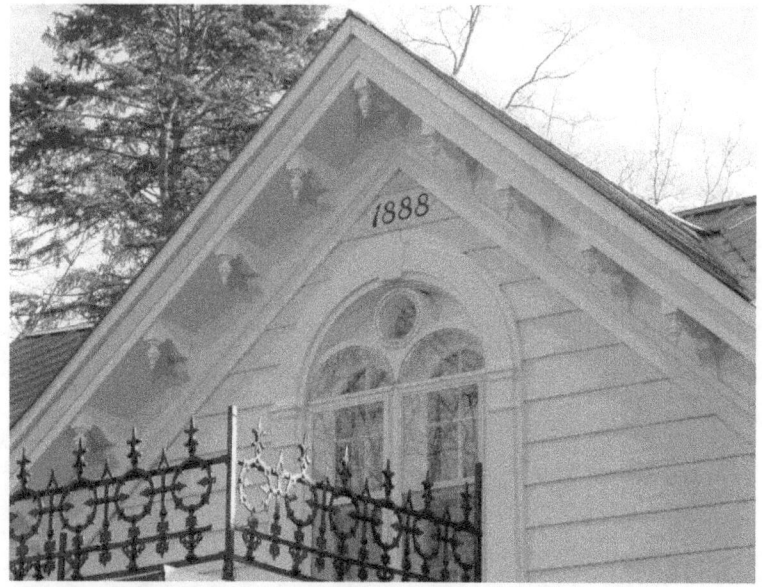

Intricate ironwork around the balcony
159 King Street

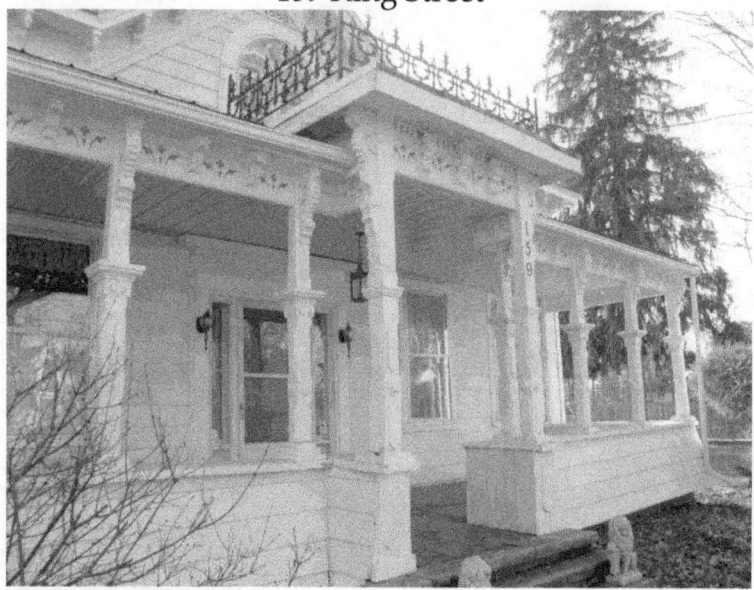

Intricate details on the brackets, pillars and below the eaves

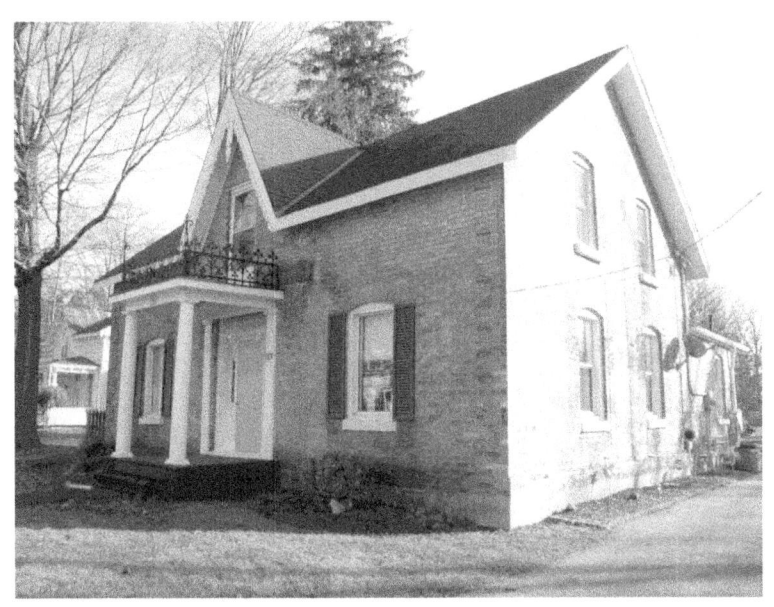

161 King Street

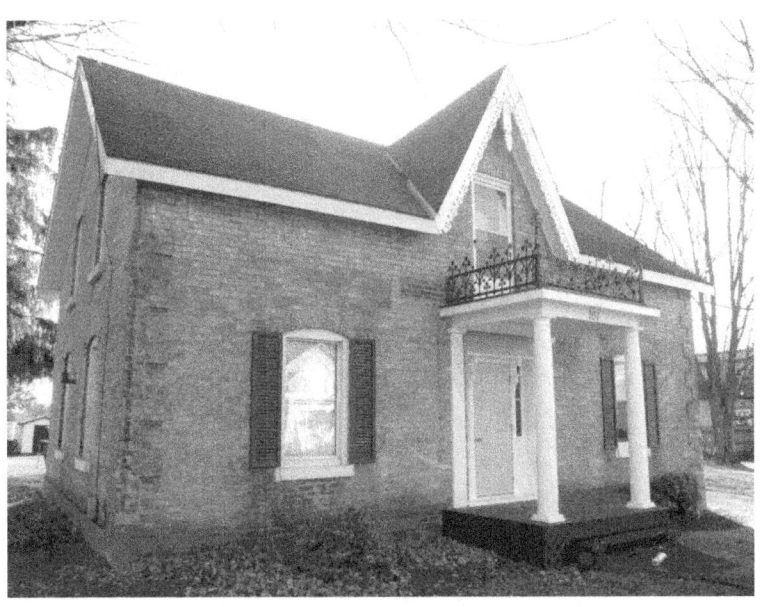

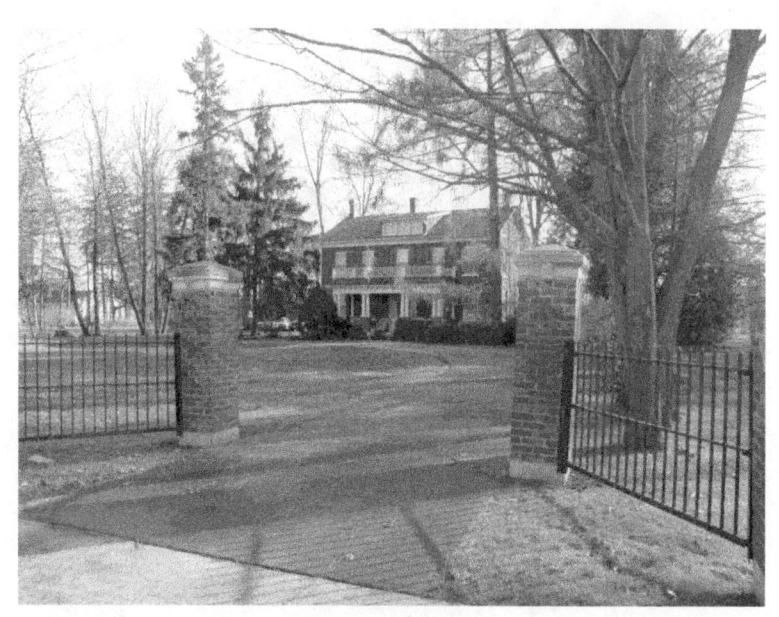

A heritage property c. 1800
155 King Street

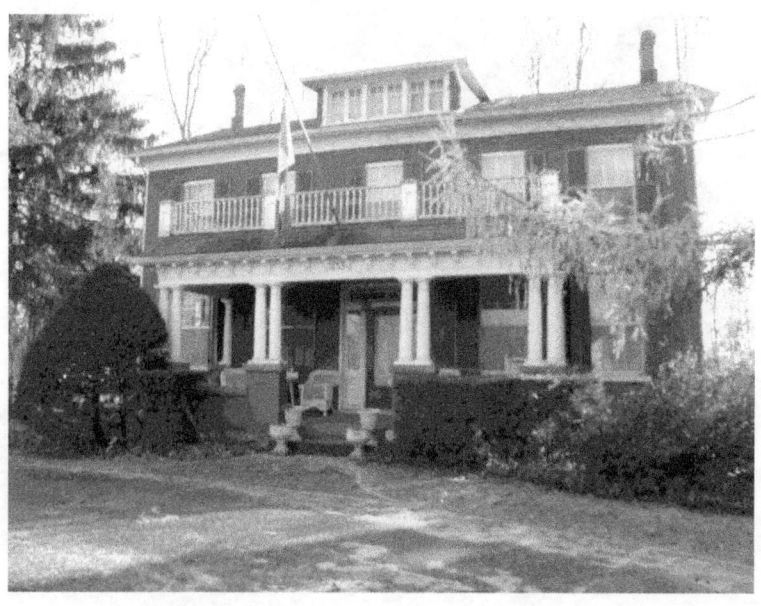

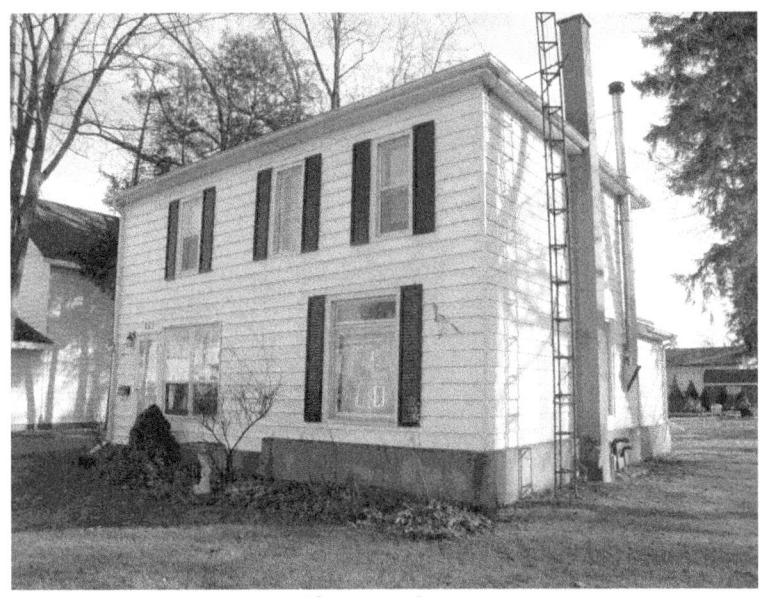

153 King Street

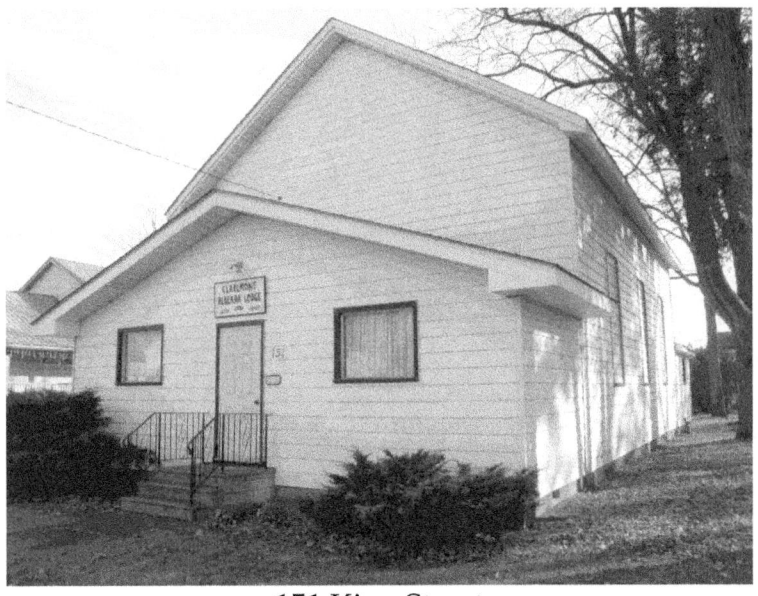

151 King Street
Claremont Rebekah Lodge

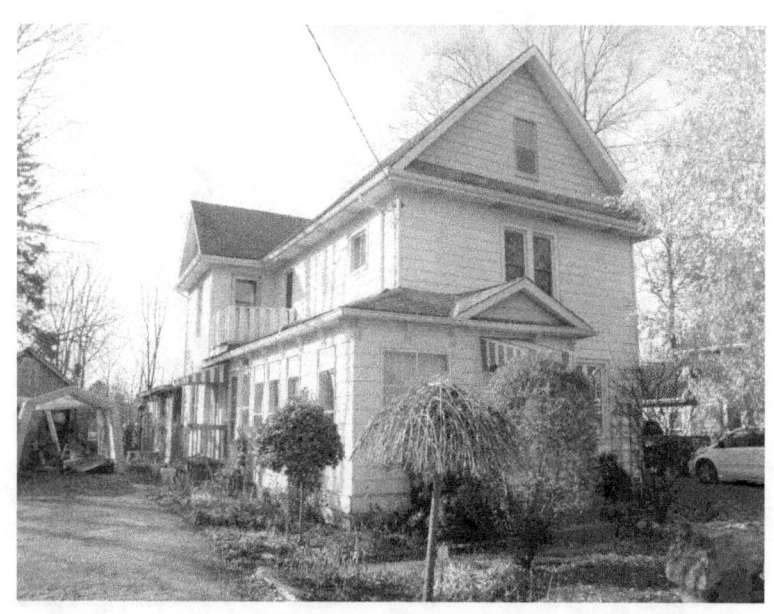

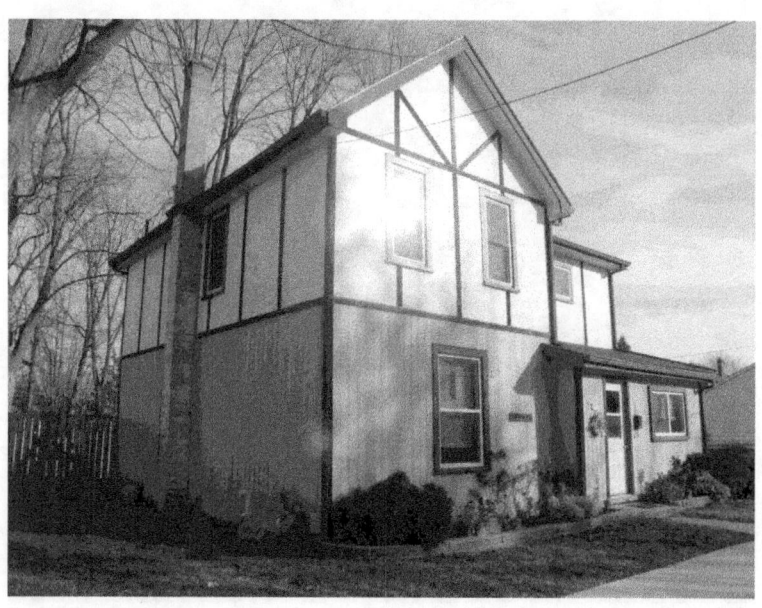

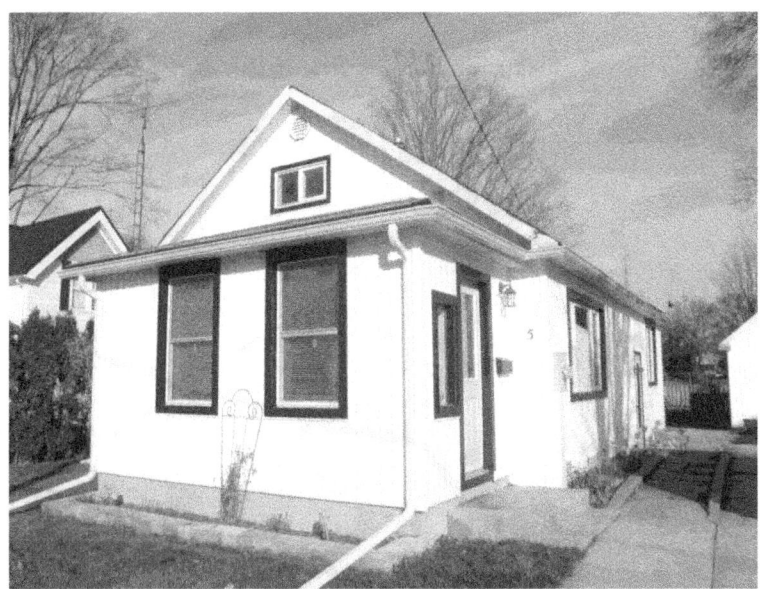

3 Saint William Street

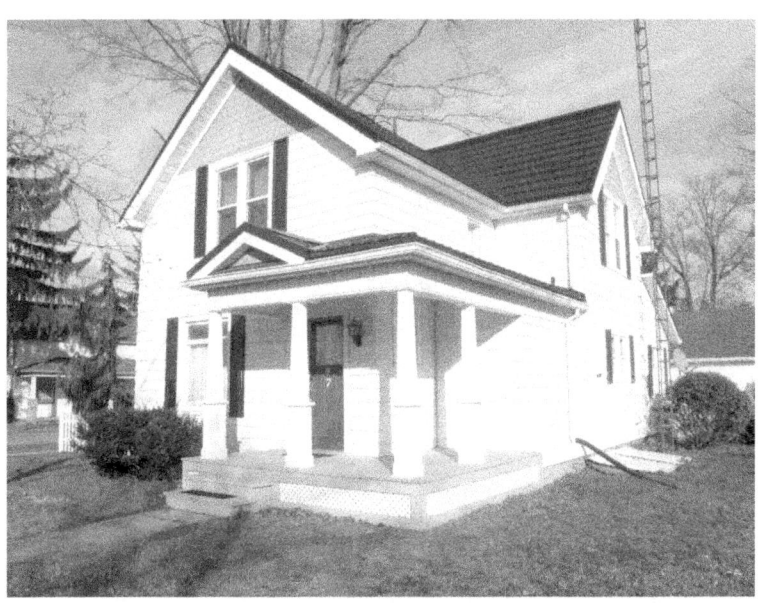

7 Saint William Street

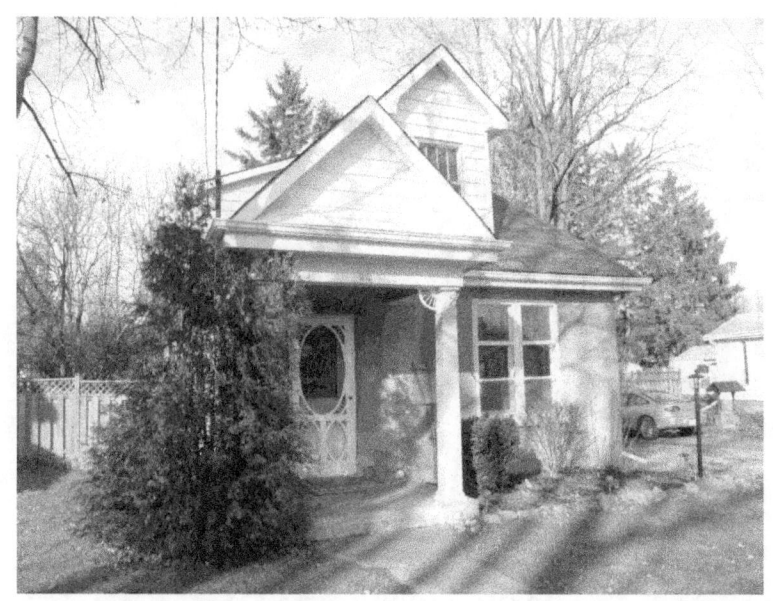

#23

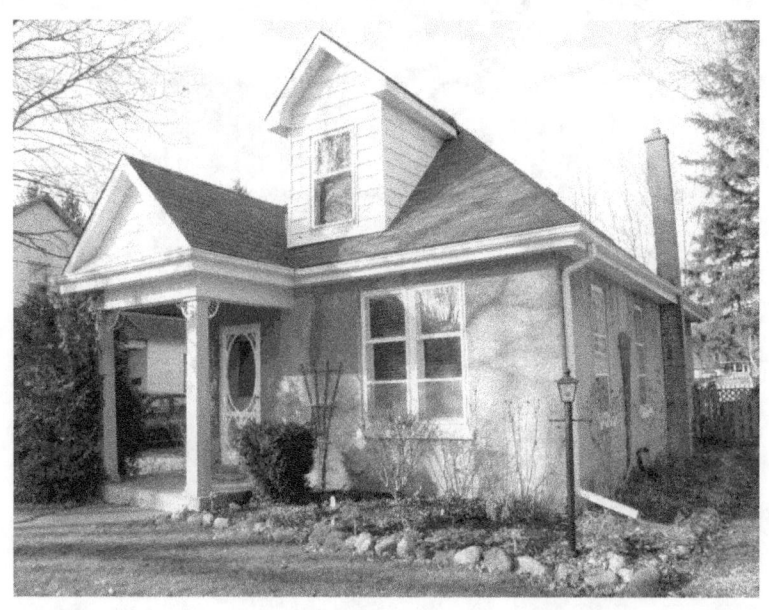

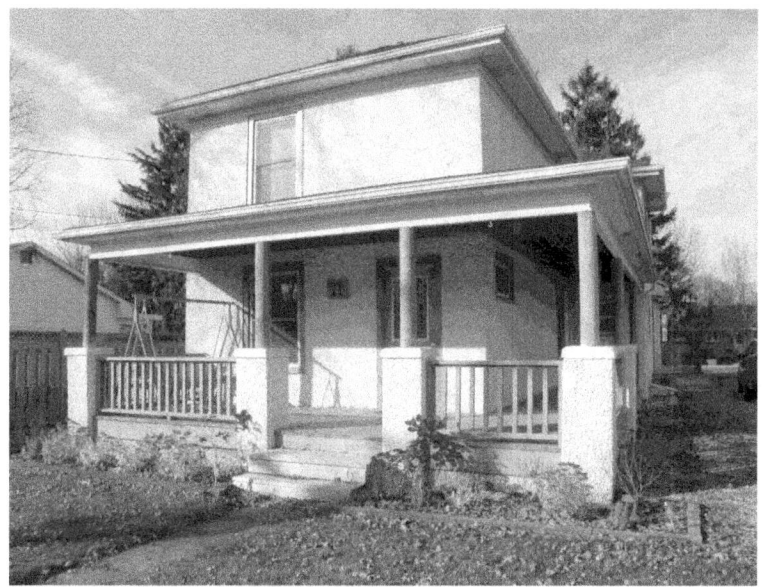

19 Dufferin Avenue

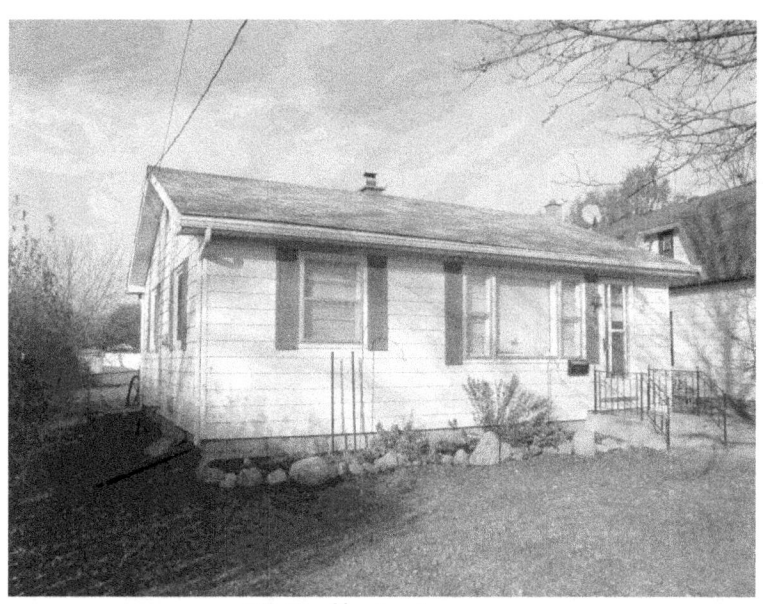

15 Dufferin Avenue

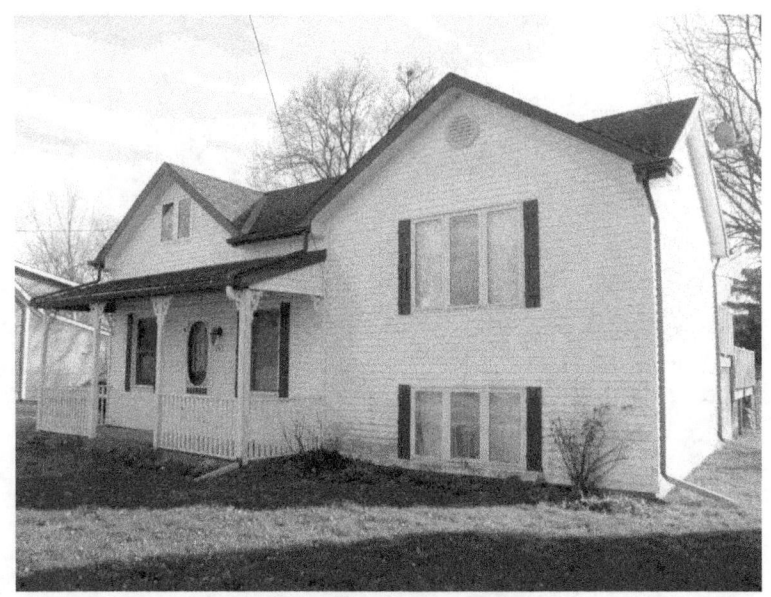

14 Dufferin Avenue

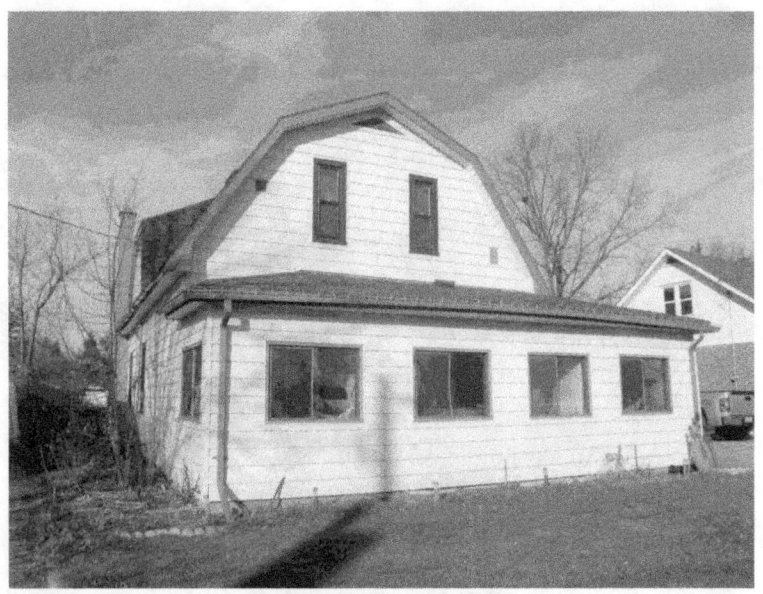

13 Dufferin Avenue

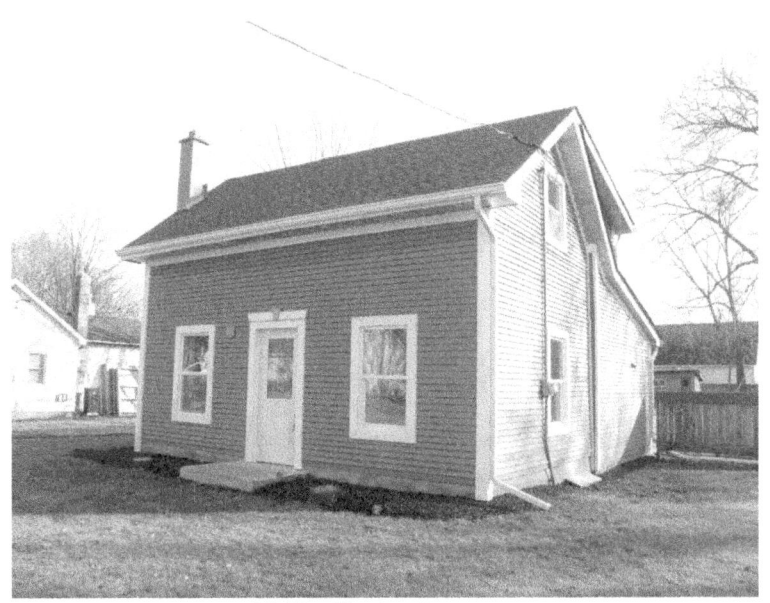

12 Dufferin Avenue

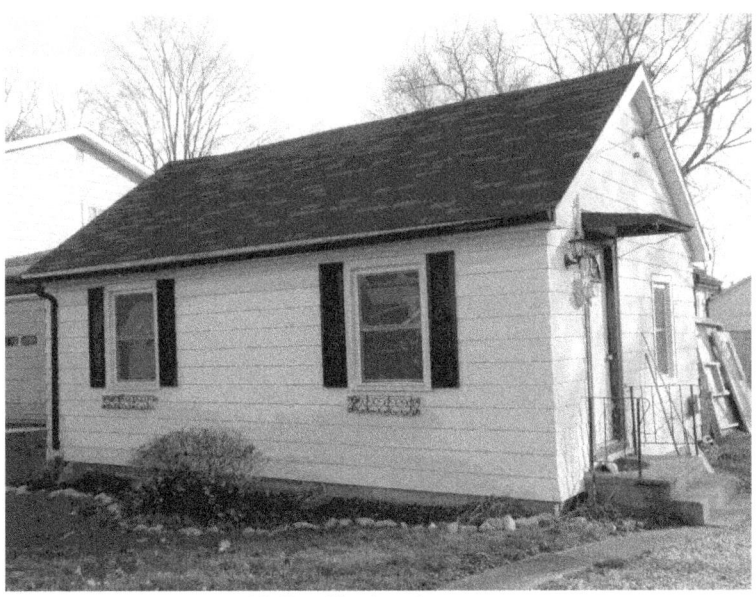

10 Dufferin Avenue

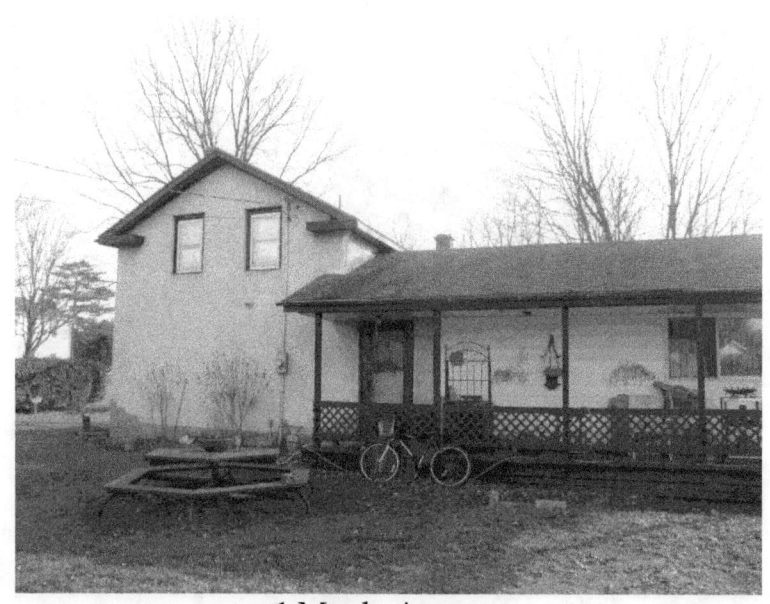

1 Maple Avenue

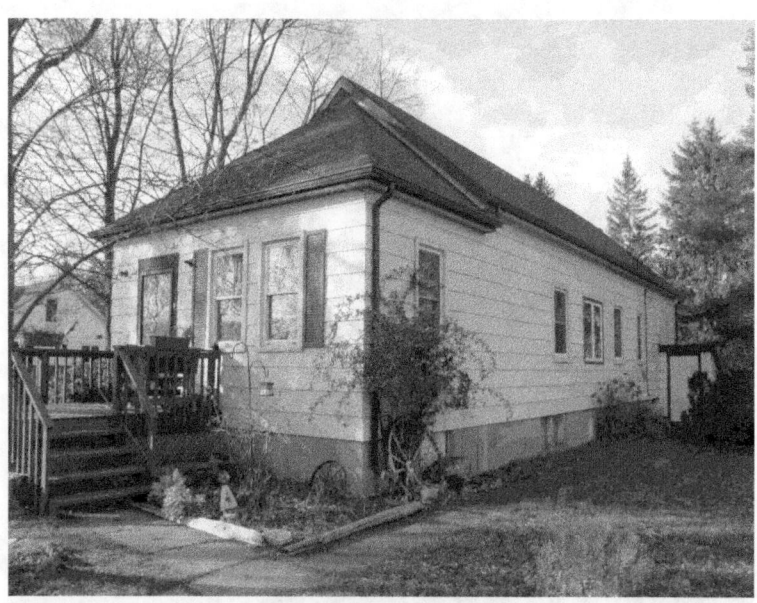

5 Maple Avenue

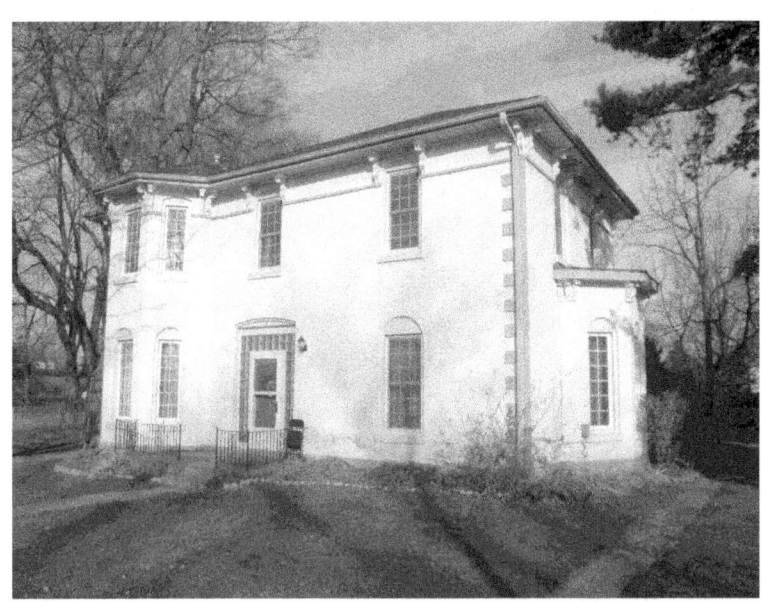

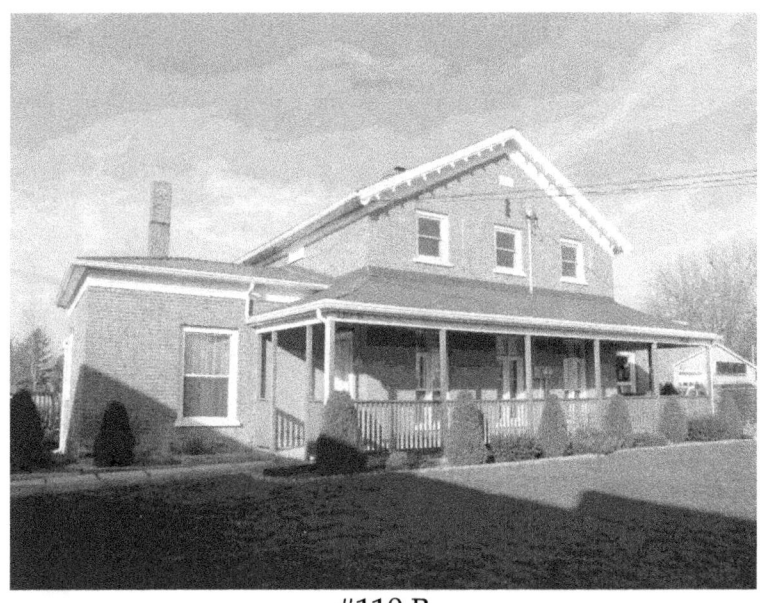

#110 B
A.D. 1851

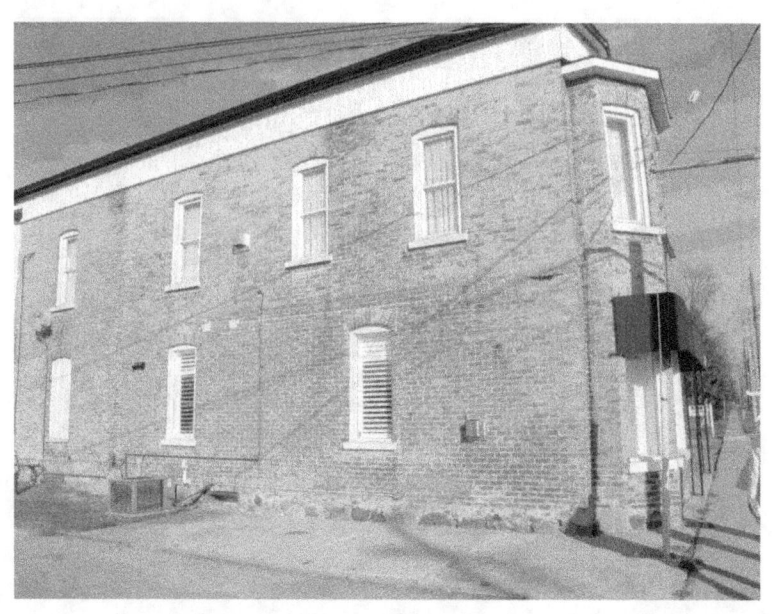

108 King Street

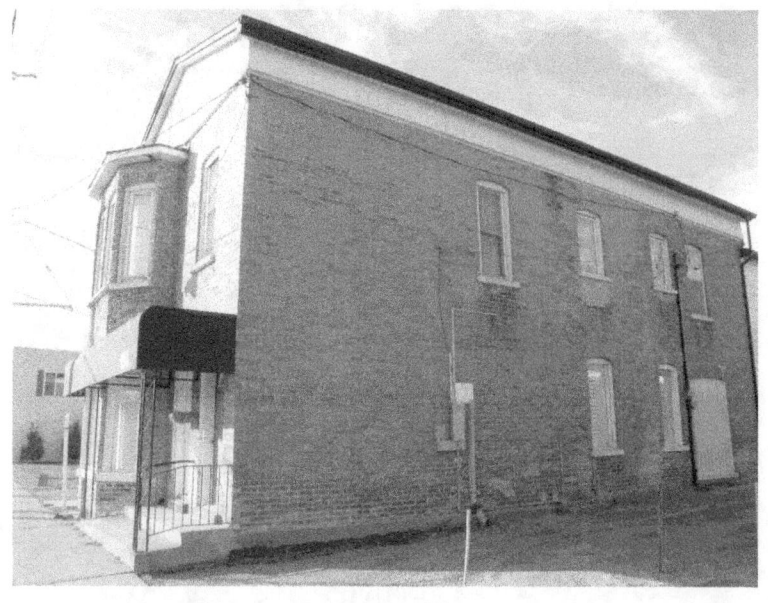

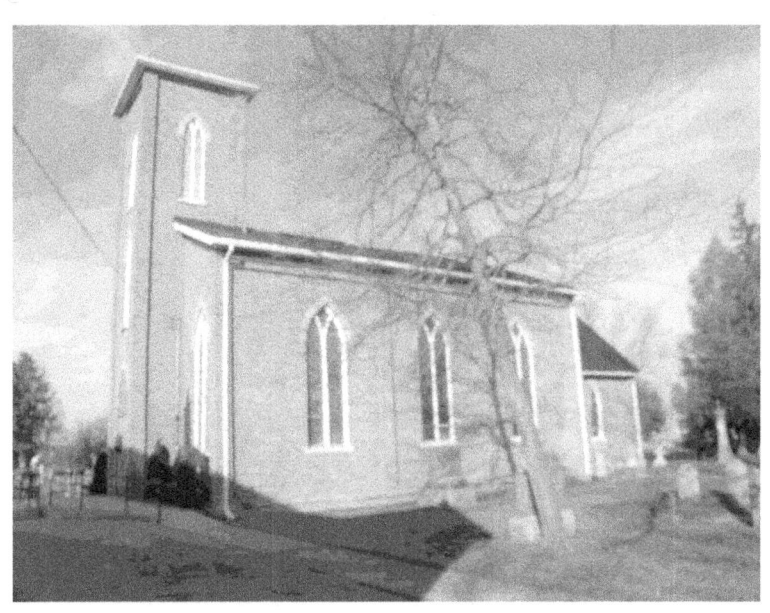

Holy Trinity Anglican Church
104 King Street

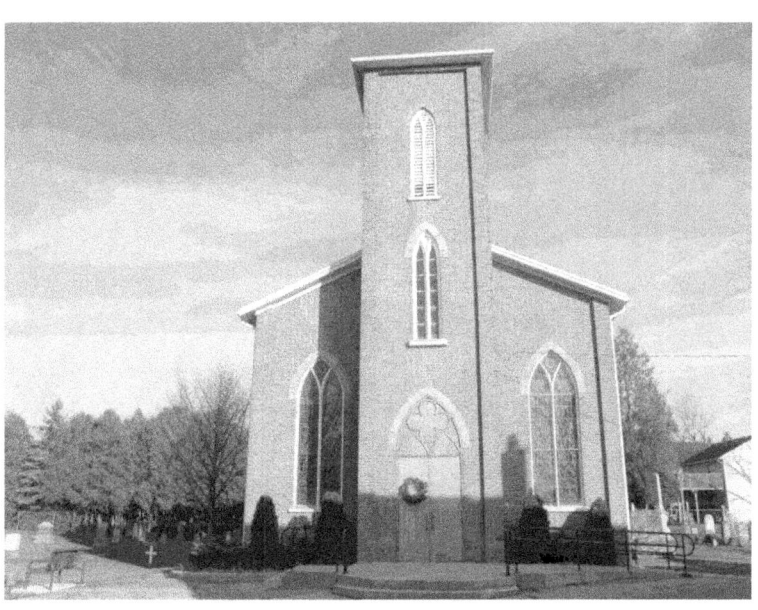

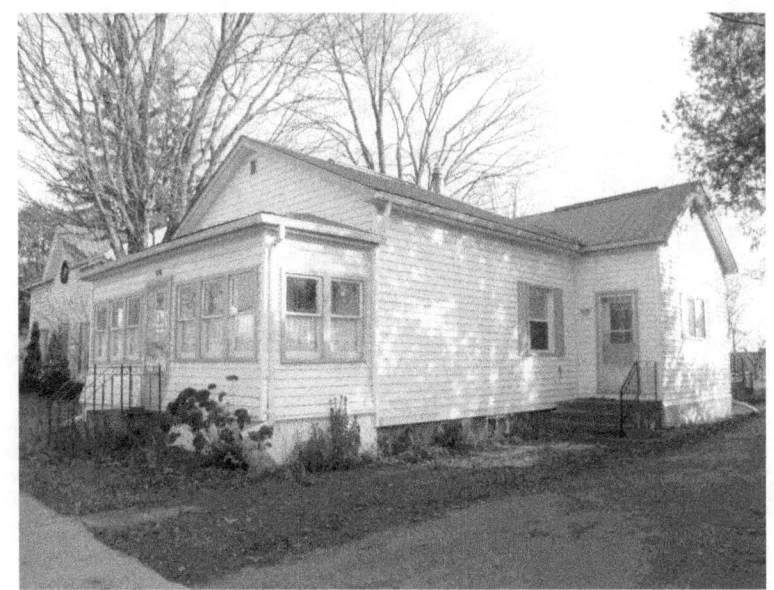

99 King Street

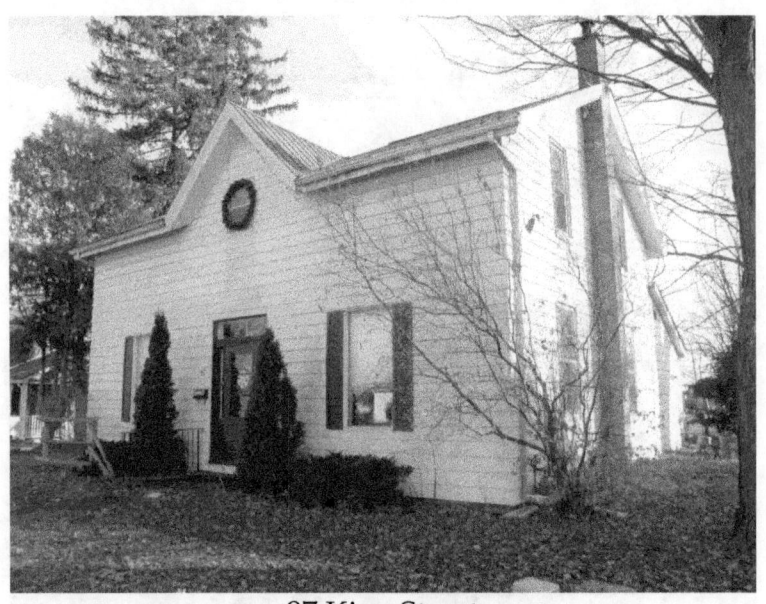

97 King Street

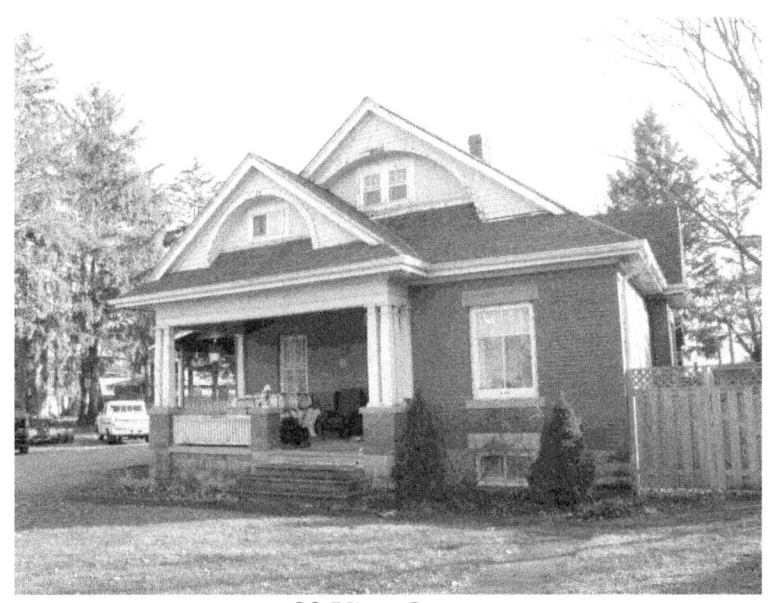

89 King Street
Heritage Property 1925

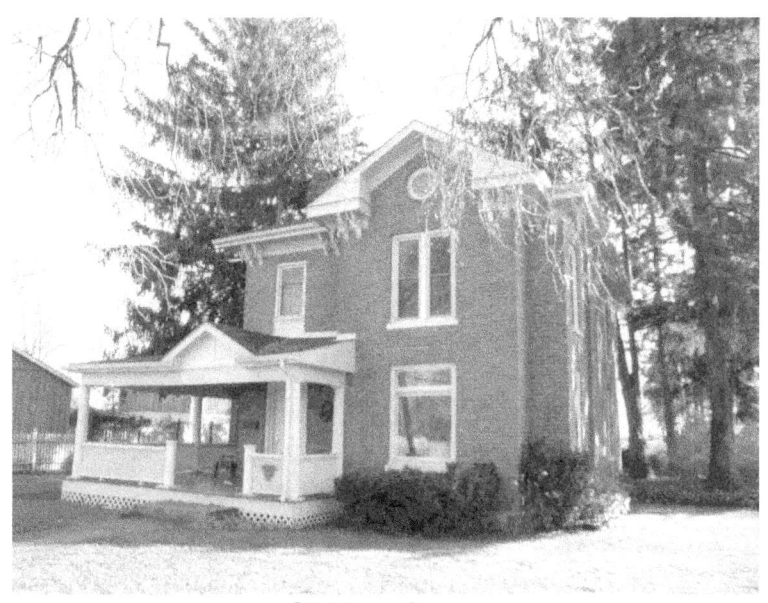

85 King Street

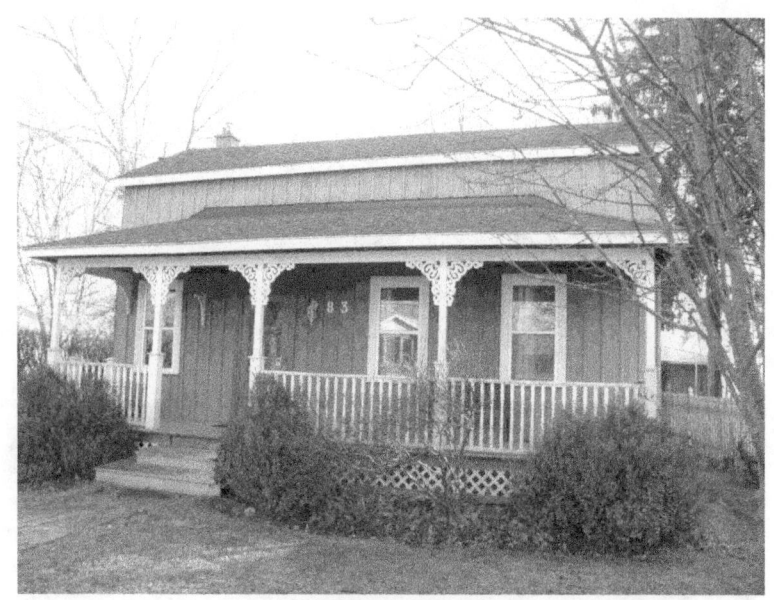

83 King Street

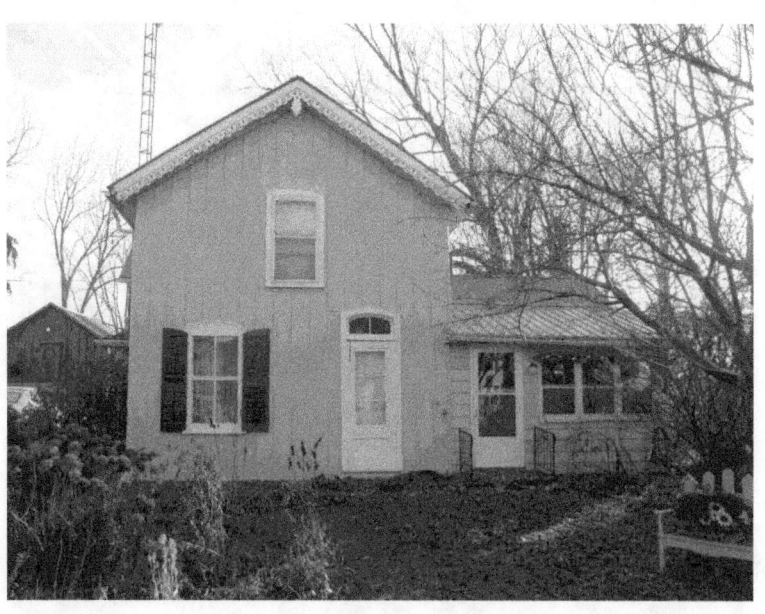

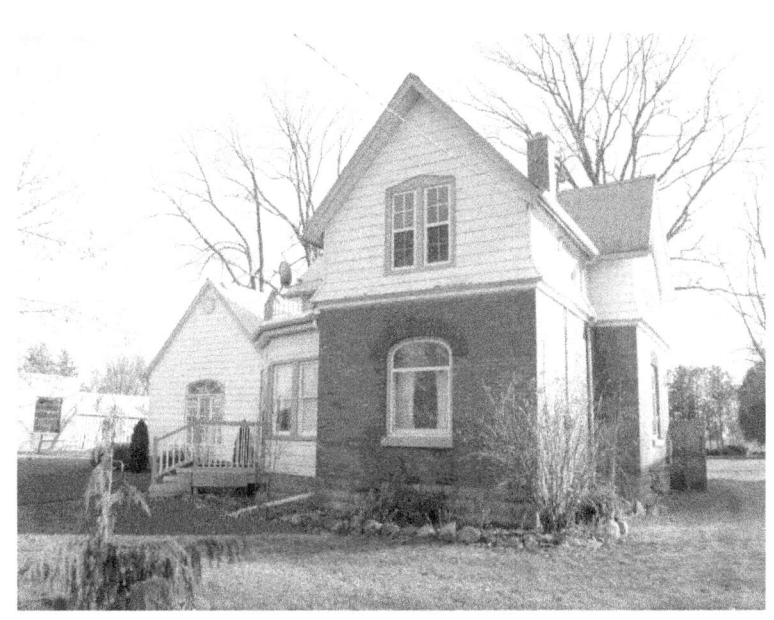

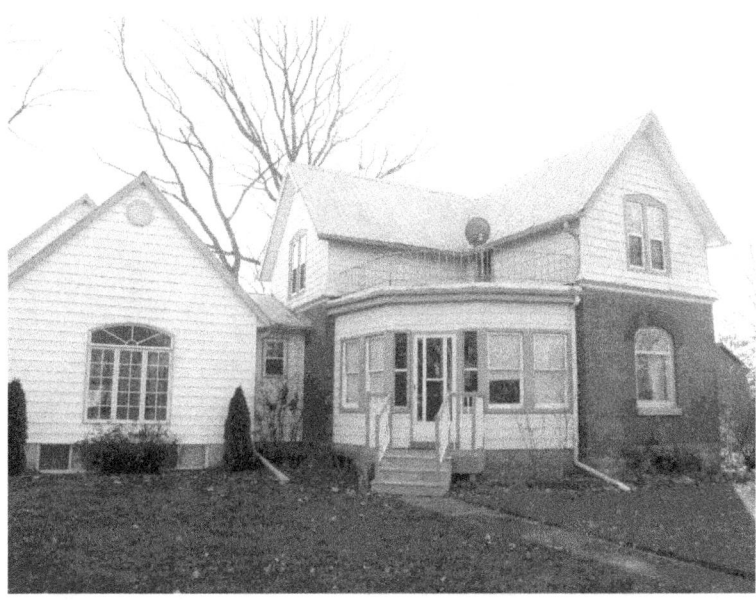

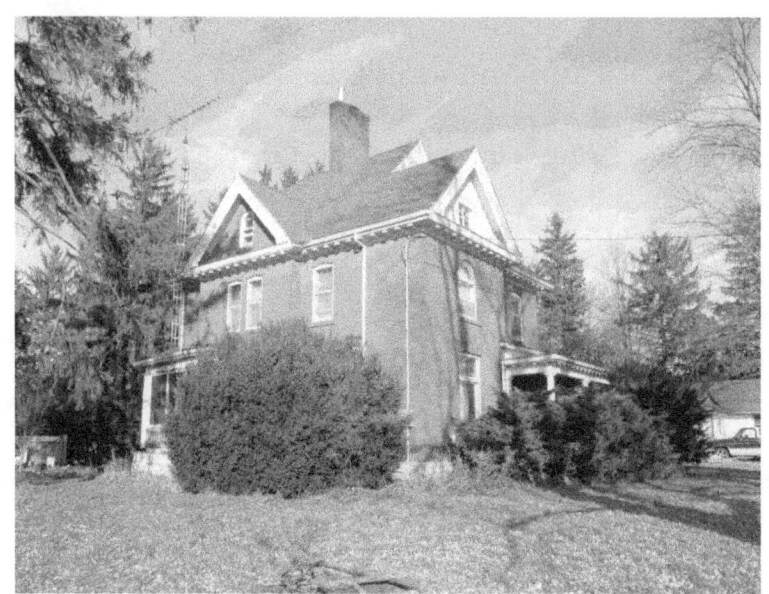

80 King Street

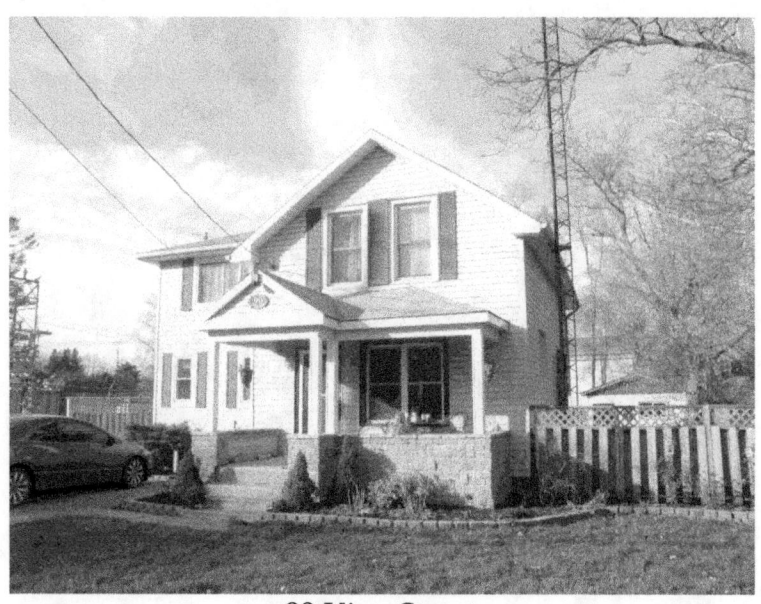

90 King Street

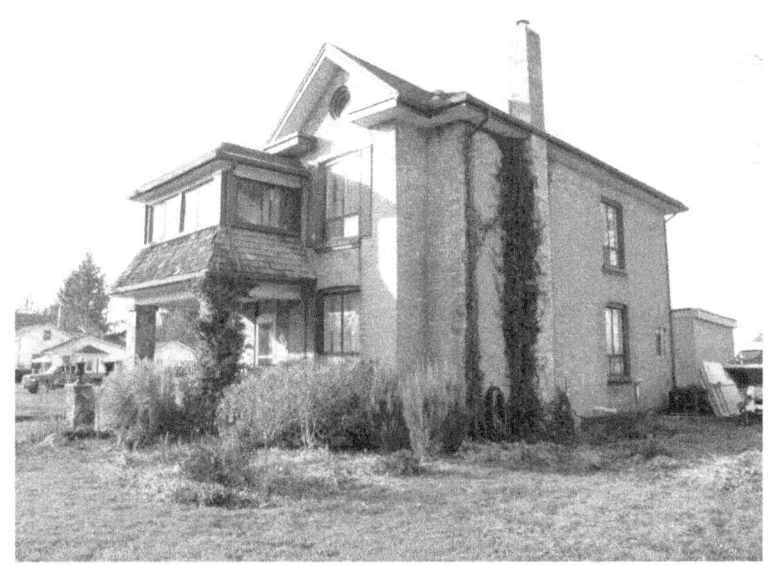

96 King Street

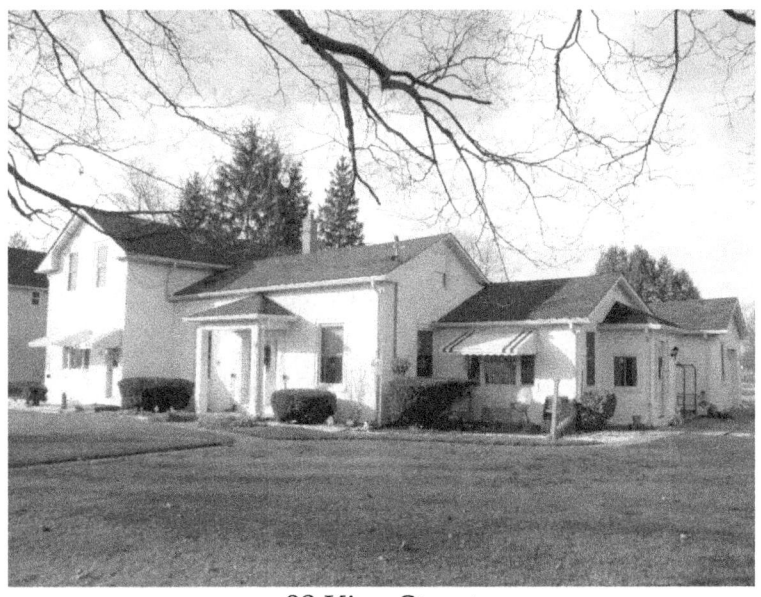

98 King Street

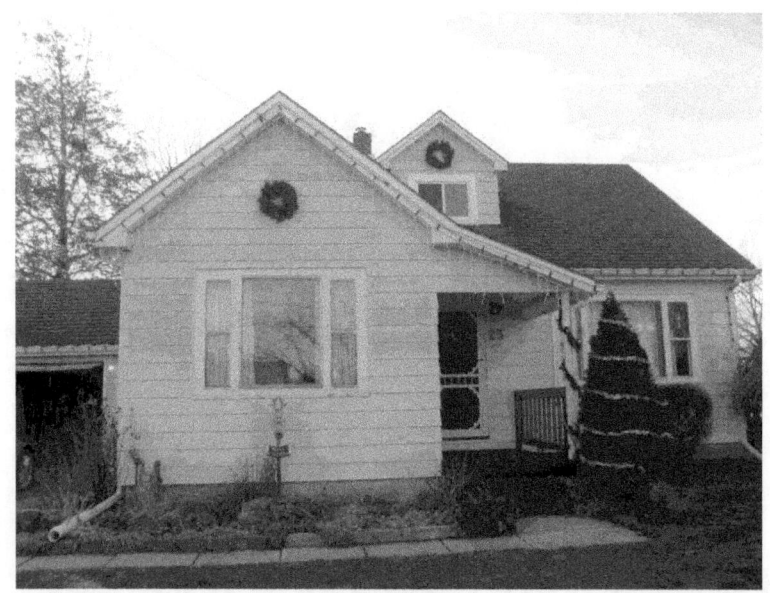

#23

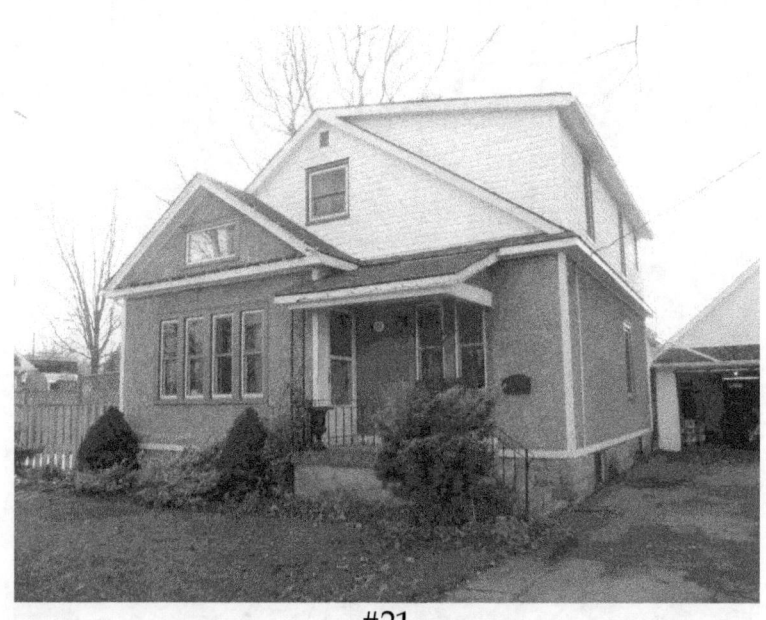

#21

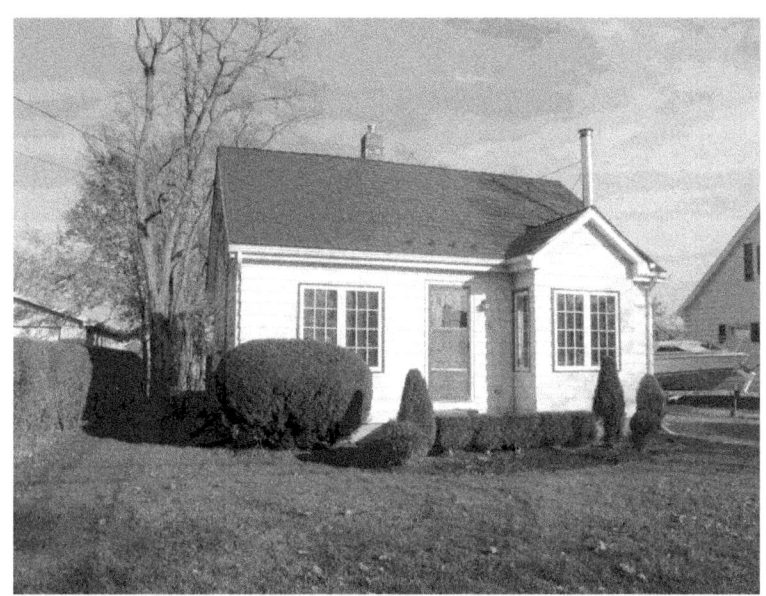

#18

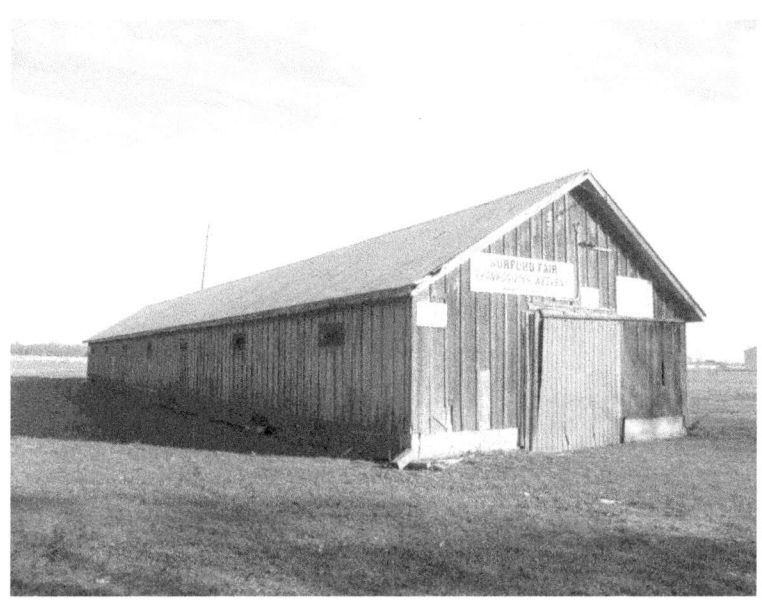

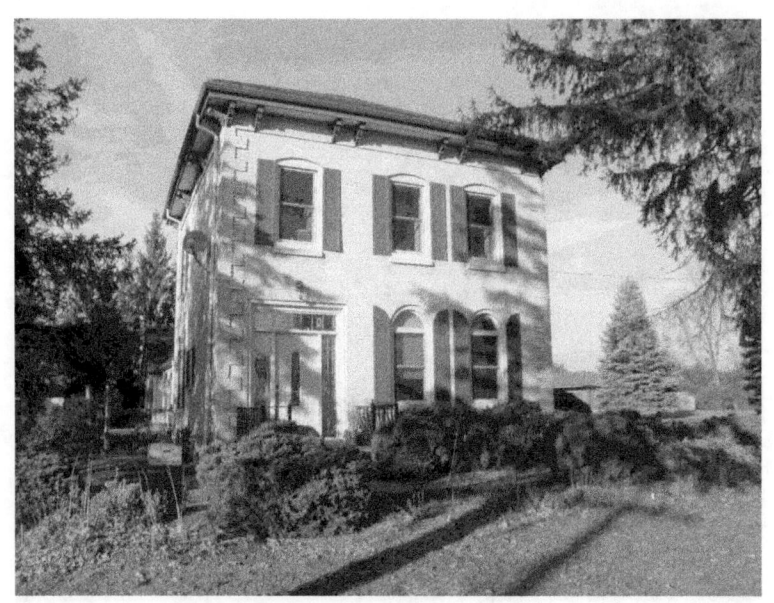

Heritage Property 1870
2 John Street

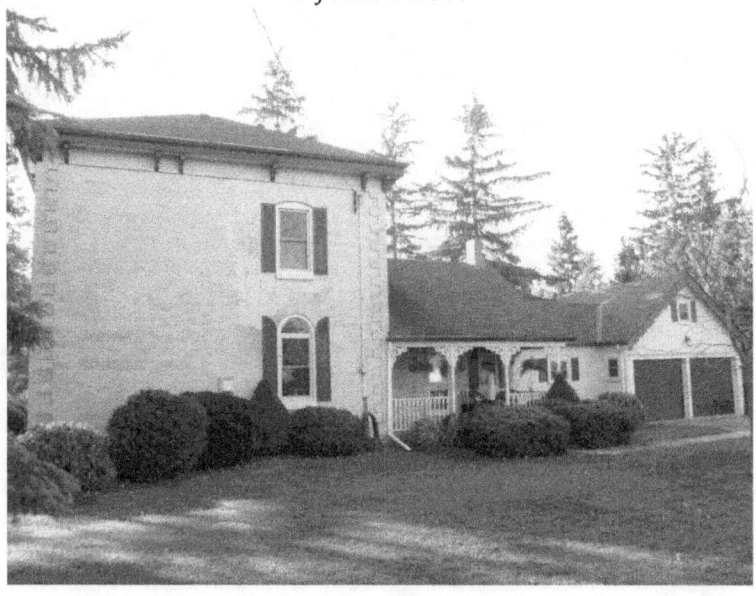

Mount Vernon

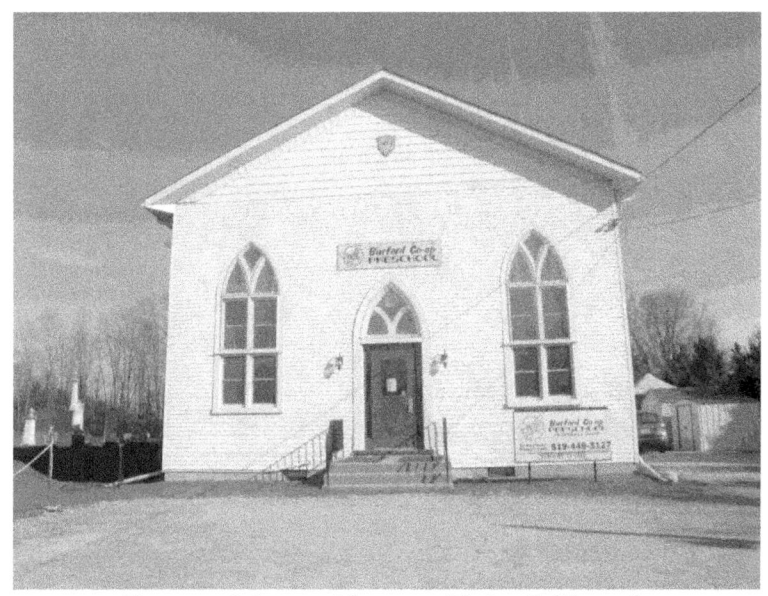

Former Mount Vernon United Church
11 Mill Street
Built in 1850

Now it is used by Burford Co-op Preschool

Bishopsgate

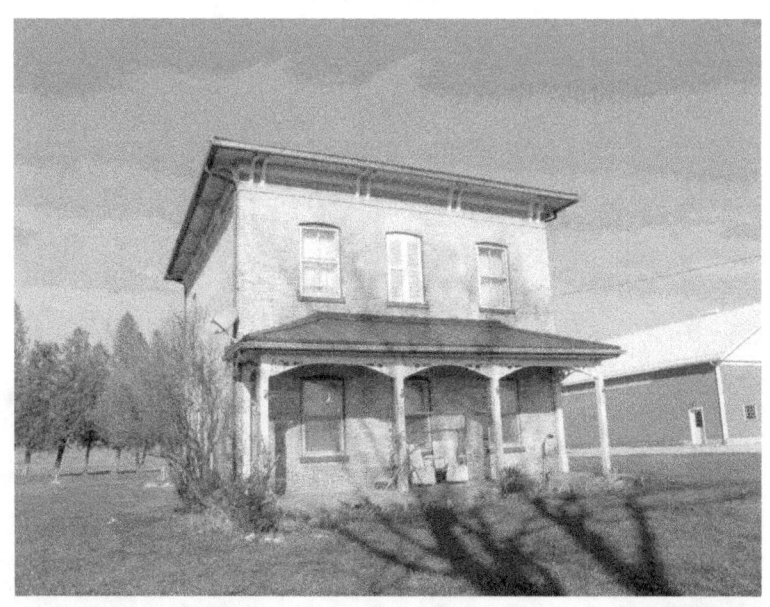

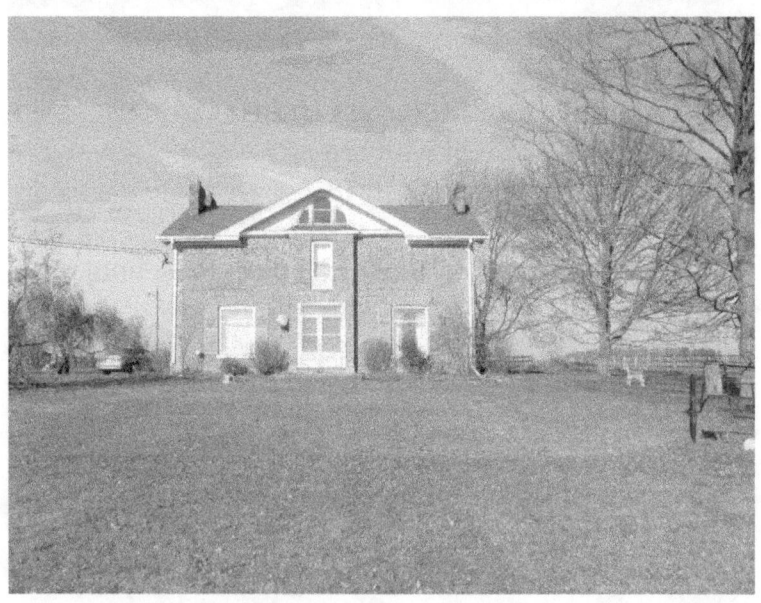